ONE FAITH,
MANY CULTURES

The Boston Theological Institute Annual Series

Volume 1   *Human Rights and the Global Mission of the Church*

The Boston Theological Institute
Annual Volume 2

ONE FAITH,
MANY CULTURES

Inculturation, Indigenization, and Contextualization

Ruy O. Costa, Editor

Orbis Books
Maryknoll, New York

Boston Theological Institute
Cambridge, Massachusetts

Manuscript Editor: William E. Jerman

Cover Photo Credits (clockwise from upper left): Steve DeMott, M.M.; Patricia Jacobsen, M.M.; D. Robinson, M.M.; Douglas Venne, M.M.; B. McCahill, M.M.

Cover Design: Catherine Figart

Library of Congress Cataloging-in-Publication Data

One faith, many cultures.

  (The Boston Theological Institute annual volume; 2)
  Includes bibliographies.
  1. Christianity and culture. 2. Jesus Christ—
Persons and offices. 3. Christianity—Developing
countries. 4. Christianity—United States.
5. Theology—Methodology. I. Costa, Ruy O. II. Series.
BR115.C8054 1988   261   87-28301
ORBIS/ISBN 0-88344-587-5
ORBIS/ISBN 0-88344-586-7 (pbk.)
BTI/ISSN 0-0885-9345

Contents

Foreword

Lorine M. Getz
Executive Director of the BTI

The Boston Theological Institute, one of the oldest and largest theological consortia in North America, is proud to present *The BTI Annual Volume 2: One Faith, Many Cultures: Inculturation, Indigenization, and Contextualization*. The theme of each annual volume is selected by its relevance to the ongoing dialogue concerning theology and the world. We hope that our publication will continue to interest and be of use to professional theologians, ministers, students of religion, the laity, and other persons concerned with global issues.

In addition to treating critically an area of importance and concern, the subject of each volume reflects the diverse character of the BTI itself. The Boston Theological Institute was conceived and incorporated in 1968 by the vision of some of the foremost ecumenists and theologians of this century. This vision is being continued today through the nine member schools: Andover Newton Theological School, Boston College Department of Theology, Boston University School of Theology, Episcopal Divinity School, Gordon-Conwell Theological Seminary, Harvard Divinity School, Holy Cross Greek Orthodox School of Theology, St. John's Seminary, and Weston School of Theology. Within these schools, more than two hundred full-time faculty members and two thousand students represent a wide range of Christian traditions and other world religions, contributing to and benefiting from a vast richness of thought, experience and exchange.

In 1988 the Boston Theological Institute celebrates its twentieth anniversary, a milestone which affirms the enduring importance of ecumenical cooperation, especially in theological education. As we look back on accomplishments, we also look forward to continuing our programs in faculty exchange, joint libraries, development, and interschool and community events, as well as our specific programs designed to address key issues in theological education, providing opportunities for all the member schools in the consortium. Examples of these unique experiences include: the International Missions and Ecumenism Program, which provides opportunities for overseas study for interested students of missions, encourages and assists the participation of international students, and organizes conferences on global issues within the world's religious communities; the Inter-religious Dialogue Program, which has expanded from its original focus on Jewish-Christian dialogue to include conversations with other world faiths such as Buddhism, Hinduism, and Islam, offering programs promoting the sharing of perspectives and understanding; the Peace and Justice Program, which hosts events and distributes information to encourage awareness regarding local and worldwide issues on peace and human rights; the Race Relations Program, which concentrates on promoting multiracial and multicultural ministries, addressing issues of racism and prejudice; and the Women in Theological Studies Program, a resource for women that addresses issues of concern to women in religion and publishes and distributes nationally a *Registry of Women in Religious Studies* and *Placement News*. All of these programs are offered with a commitment to maintaining an interdenominational focus, and to providing a type of education that will enable graduates to develop cooperative leadership in religious and social communities.

The BTI Annual Series was inaugurated in the spring of 1986, with the publication of *Volume 1: Human Rights and the Global Mission of the Church*. With this volume, the BTI is pleased to announce a co-publishing relationship for the series with Orbis Books, a leader in publishing works of theological importance.

Volume 2 is the consolidation of a dialogue which took place on March 21 and 22, 1986. Faculty and students from the member schools of the BTI attended and participated in a conference addressing the subject of "Contextualization of the Faith: Past, Present, and Future." Many of the presentations made at this conference are collected into this volume. However, the contributions of all the participants are appreciated, for they enhanced the richness of the event and this subsequent volume as a whole. In addition, special thanks are due to Ruy Costa, who coordinated the conference and edited this volume, and to Diana Small, Ellen Brenner, and Lydia Barton, who assisted in the production of this volume.

Introduction:
Inculturation, Indigenization, and Contextualization

Ruy O. Costa
Editor of the Second Annual BTI Volume

Sahid waited by the side of the river for years—some say ten, some twenty, others even thirty . . . At length Bonang returned and saw that Sahid . . . had indeed been steadfast. But instead of teaching him the doctrines of Islam he merely said, "You have been a good pupil, and as a result of your long meditation you now know more than I do," and he began to ask him questions, advanced questions, on religious matters, which the uninstructed pupil answered immediately and correctly. Bonang then gave him his new name, Kalidjaga—"he who guards the river"—and told him to go forth and spread the doctrine of Islam, which he then did with unsurpassed effectiveness [Geertz, 29].

Inculturation, indigenization, and contextualization are distinct and related concepts. Because they are related and because they point to dynamic cultural and social phenomena, they are often used synonymously. This use, however, deflates their peculiarities. What follows is a brief introduction to their distinctions and relatedness. Kalidjaga in Indonesia and Luysi in Morocco illustrate the process of inculturation of Islam in two different environments.

Kalidjaga, regarded as the apostle who introduced Islam to Java, was converted through a powerful encounter with Bonang, a Muslim teacher. Clifford Geertz observes that Kalidjaga "had become a Muslim without ever having seen the Koran, entered a mosque or heard a prayer—through an inner change of heart brought by the same sort of yoga-like psychic discipline that was the core of the Indic tradition from which he came" (Geertz, 29). He symbolizes a bridge between the Javanese Indic background and its Islamic civilization. It was his Madjapahit Hindu-Buddhism that made it possible for him to become an apostle of Islam. At the same time, the Islam reproduced and legitimated by his experience was one made in the image and likeness of that Indic background (Geertz, 54). In the old Madjapahit tradition, Kalidjaga is an example of and an exemplar for Javanese Islam.

Geertz compares Kalidjaga to a Moroccan saint, Abu Ali Al-Hasan ben Masud Al-Yusi, known as Sidi Lahesen Lyusi, who was a disciple of the pre-Saharan Sufi Sheik Ahmed ben Nazir Al-Dari, the founder of the order of the Naziri, "still quite important in Morocco" (Geertz, 32). Lyusi's life story is a paradigm of courage, loyalty, moral intensity, adventure, and the like, which are values prized by Moroccan Islam (Geertz, 33).

After careful examination of the socio-cultural environments which sanctified the experiences of these two radically different leaders, Geertz concludes that the conception of what life is all about, "a conception which they call Islamic," means substantially different things to these two cultures:

> On the Indonesian side, inwardness, imperturbability, patience, poise, sensibility, elitism, and an almost obsessive self-effacement, the radical dissolution of individuality; on the Moroccan side, activism, fervor, impetuosity, nerve, toughness, moralism, populism, and an almost obsessive self-assertion, the radical intensification of individuality [Geertz, 54].

The point is obvious: Islam is not quite the same in Morocco and Indonesia.

Some advocates of inculturation, indigenization or contextualization claim to find their paradigm in the Bible itself. Saul, the Pharisee who became Paul in order to preach to the gentiles, for example, quoted Greek poetry as the Word of God to Greeks in order to convert Greeks.

The evangelistic efforts of Bartolomé de las Casas in Central America, José de Anchieta in Brazil, Roberto de Nobili in India, and many others mark the beginning of the contemporary reflection on our topic. In India this reflection was revitalized in the last century with the struggles between native leaders and foreign missionaries over church leadership, which followed the political movement against British domination in 1857, known as the "First War of Independence" (Baago, 1). In the 1850's, Lal Behari Day, an Indian pastor and writer, started a movement against the missionary domination of the church. He advocated equal status for Indian ordained ministers vis-à-vis the missionaries (Baago, 2). In 1868 a number of Indian leaders founded the Bengal Christian Association for the Promotion of Christian Truth and Godliness, and the Protection of the Rights of Indian Christians. The first president of the association was Krishna Mohun Banerja (Baago, 2). A few years later a missionary blamed the association for fostering "bitterness, suspicion and even dislike" toward European missionaries and for administering "hard knocks" to the missionaries and their policies (Baago, 4–8). Afterward a number of organizations were created with the purpose of developing an independent Indian church (Baago, 4–8). In 1877 the Bengali Christian Conference was organized; in 1887 the Calcutta Christo Samaj; and in 1886 the National Church of Madras.

Krishna Mohun Banerja is the author of *The Arian Witness: or Testimony of Arian Scriptures in Corroboration of Biblical History and the Rudiments of Christian Doctrine, including dissertations on the original home and early adventures of Indo-Arians* (Calcutta: 1875), a system of Christian apologetics in relation to the Vedic religion. His argument is that Christianity is the logical conclusion of original Hinduism and the fulfillment of the early Vedic writings. In "Christ the true Prajapathi" he traces a parallel between the Vedic idea of the sacrifice of *purusha* with the death of Christ:

> The Vedic writers say distinctly that the Lord of Creation, himself a Purusha begotten in the beginning (or before all worlds) offered himself a sacrifice for the Devas, who by birth were mortals like men, but were translated to heaven "by path of sacrifice". They add that the same Lord of Creation was "half mortal, half immortal". This is still nearer an approach to the ideal of our Immanuel [Banerja, 1880:90].

More than once Banerja makes the point that "no other person than Jesus of Nazareth has ever appeared in the world claiming the character and position of the self-sacrificing Prajapathi" (Banerja, 1892:1–2) and, therefore, Jesus is the true Prajapathi of the Vedas.

Banerja also finds parallels between the Old Testament and the Vedic accounts of creation and fall, the flood, and so forth. His pan-Babilonist examination of Assyrian and Vedic texts leads him to the conclusion that the original home of the Arians had been Media. For him this accounts for the similarity between the sacrificial systems of Genesis and the Vedas (Banerja, 1880:69ff.). This is a crucial connection since it points to the centrality of sacrifice in both the biblical and Vedic traditions.

Banerja's agenda is the evangelization of Hindus with an appeal to the most ancient tradition of the Brahminical Arians of India, the authors of the Vedas and their primitive ancestors. In the Introduction to *The Arian Witness* he writes:

> We look to our Witness . . . for the disproof of an idea often broached against Hindu Christians that they are rebels against the *sanatana* dharma of the country, and apostates from the faith that has animated the Hindu mind, and the rule of life that has governed Hindu practice, from time immemorial [Banerja, 1875:10].

The central point of Banerja's thesis is that, far from being a foreign religion, Christianity is the true fulfillment of the Vedas. A Hindu can be a good Hindu and a good Christian at the same time.

In 1955 the East Asia Theological Commission set up by the World Council

of Churches (WCC) organized the Bangalore Conference on the Indigenization of Worship. Two main sets of issues were debated in Bangalore: at the
institutional level, advocates of indigenization were concerned with the organizational domination of the churches in mission fields by foreign missionaries;
at the level of the theological/cultural encounter, advocates of indigenization
argued for culture-sensitive interpretations of the Christian faith. Third World
indigenizers claimed that a living theology is much more than the translation of
credal and confessional formulas. Robert Schreiter collects a number of
illustrations of cross-cultural dilemmas met by Western missionaries: what was
the Catholic Church to do with celibacy in cultures "where not to marry and
have children was a way of cursing one's parents" (Schreiter, 3)? Or how to
baptize Masai women in East Africa "where to pour water on the head of a
woman was to curse her with infertility" (Schreiter, 2)?

The most visible issue at this level of the debate is the problem of cross-
cultural communication. A less visible but equally critical and sometimes even
more threatening issue is the problem of the content to be communicated.
Charles Kraft says that the purpose of communication is "to bring a receptor to
understand a message presented by a communicator in a way that substantially
corresponds with the intent of the communicator" (Kraft, 147). In the debates
over indigenization, the occupation with cross-cultural translation of the faith
implied a preoccupation with one's interpretation of that same faith. Indigenization meant the translation into "native" cultures of a *Missio Dei* previously
adopted by the missionary. In Bangalore Indian theologians "realized that the
Gospel had been brought to India from countries where the seed had already
been subjected to an indigenization" (Lash, 25).

The concept of contextualization was introduced in 1972 by the WCC in
response to the need for reform in theological education. The difference
between indigenization and contextualization is stated in *Ministry in Context*,
published by the WCC Theological Education Fund (TEF):

> Indigenization tends to be used in the sense of responding to the Gospel in
> terms of a traditional culture. Contextualization, while not ignoring this,
> takes into account the process of secularism, technology and the struggle
> for human justice, which characterizes the historical moment of nations
> in the Third World [*Ministry in Context*, 20].

Inculturation, indigenization, and contextualization are evangelistic-
apologetic concepts; inculturation and indigenization are apologetic methods
focused on the translation/interpretation of a received text for a given culture,
whereas contextualization sees this translation/interpretation as a dialectical
process in which text and context are interdependent. The agenda of the first
paradigm is what German theologians baptized as "history of salvation";
the agenda of the second is what, since Uppsala 1968 has been called "salvation in history" (Conn, 93). In this case, most of "Christian civilization" still
needs to be evangelized. At this point, true contextualization means de-

contextualization—that is, a self-critical effort at hearing the "Christ of culture" as "Christ against culture."

The importance of the historical context of the church for its interpretation of the faith brings a whole new web of issues into the complex discipline of hermeneutics. The neo-Kantian idealism of the grammatico-historical method is no longer sufficient; it is not enough, in our historical environment, to understand what the intention of the sacred writers was in theirs. Contextualization invites polemical disciplines—such as theology, social philosophy, and the social sciences—to an interdisciplinary reflection. Such a reflection, however, is not without methodological puzzles and dilemmas, such as:

1. The axiological place of the disciplines involved: Does any of these disciplines have priority over the others? Which one? Would not such priority violate the integrity of the other disciplines? Is a dialogical approach possible?
2. Intradisciplinary debates: structural vs. functional social science; dynamic vs. static views of culture; cultural diffusionism vs. developmentalism; anthropological vs. sociological or economical focuses; Weberian vs. Marxian analysis, and so on.
3. The circle of questions raised from the self-critical method itself: Is not contextualization a child of Western rationalized religion?[1] (Secularism and technology are exports of the rationalized First World.) How to balance an affirmation of an indigenous culture and the messianic drive of the contextual approach? How to avoid, on the one hand, the Geist of conquest and domination of past missionary practice and theory and, on the other hand, the laissez-faire religion of Western rationalized culture, which has in its logical consistency with religious freedom a built-in bias against prophetic preaching and practice?

Obviously a complete examination of the possible range of answers to these questions is not possible in the space allotted to this Introduction. The intention here is to invite advocates and critics of contextualization to a conversation about some of these issues. This is an invitation to self-critical reflection. Kalidjaga and Lyusi are illustrations of how inculturation happens without any conscious effort on the part of the religious community. Krishna Mohun Banerja's uncritical use of pan-Babilonist theory betrays his dependence on cultural diffusionist assumptions, and his appeal to Brahminical authority betrays an elitist soul.[2] Both instances illustrate the dialectical tension between the conscious, rational effort at indigenization on the one hand and the persistence of (unconscious) inculturation on the other.

In summary: discussions on inculturation focus on the symbolic exchange between the faith being preached and the receiving culture. Debates over indigenization include this cultic agenda but go a step further with the inclusion of conscious power struggles between foreign missionaries and national leaders. Reflections on contextualization represent a third level of interpretation of the faith, in which, to the cultic aspects and the intrachurch power struggles is added a process of conscientization about power struggles in the world, in which the church participates either actively or passively.

"Contextualizing the Faith: Past, Present, and Future" was the topic assigned to the participants in the Second Annual BTI Consultation on the Global Mission of the Church held at Andover Newton Theological School on March 21 and 22, 1986. Sixteen papers covering methodological issues, inputs from the Third and the First Worlds, practical developments within the BTI, Christology, and the like, were presented and discussed. Most of those papers are now made available to a larger audience through this edition of the BTI annual volume.

At the consultation two papers were presented as opening plenary addresses: Max Stackhouse, "Contextualization, Contextuality, and Contextualism," and Jane Cary Peck, "A Critical Contextual Approach to the Social Function of Religions: Mission, Imperialism, and Accompaniment." Stackhouse discusses the contemporary confusion over differences between the translation and indigenization of (especially, religious and theological) ideas, the fact that all important ideas are conditioned by the context in which they develop, and are often dialectically interactive with contexts other than those in which they first developed, the thesis that ideas are epiphenomenal reflections of the socio-cultural contexts in which they occur. A focal question in his paper is: "How do we know a 'context' when we see one?" How is it to be described, delimited in time, space, and social range?

Peck focuses on the Central American context where Christians are found on all sides of revolutionary struggles. She examines the influences of history, social location, and theology on Christian responses to those struggles. She compares the positions adopted by conservative Protestantism in the nonrevolutionary situation of historically democratic Costa Rica with the liberationist position of Christians in the struggles for liberation in El Salvador, Guatemala, and Honduras, and the revolutionary situation of Nicaragua's national reconstruction and struggles against the United States-backed counterrevolutionary war.

The two papers which follow are historical studies. "Christ as the Divine Guru in the Theology of Roberto de Nobili" was written by Francis Clooney. In this paper the pioneer of inculturation in India is described as "quite radical if judged according to the cultural norms of Europe in the seventeenth century" and "quite conservative when his attitude toward Hinduism as a religion and toward ideas foreign to seventeenth century Catholicism is examined." De Nobili draws a line between cultural and religious adaptation, and will not cross that line. Clooney asks whether it is possible "to go further than de Nobili did" and what limits/demands does the very idea of "mission" put on the person attempting to be as sympathetic as possible to non-Christians.

Francis Sullivan's contribution, "The Formation of a Missionary: Bartolomé de las Casas, 1484–1566," is based especially on Las Casas' work *On the Only Way to Draw Anyone to the Truth of Salvation*, wherein the sixteenth century missionary to Central America documents his struggles, first against the enslavement of Amerindians, and later against the enslavement of Africans. Sullivan's style is a warm invitation to a spiritual communion with the evangelic heart of Las Casas, a communion which Sullivan enjoys almost like a disciple in awe, certainly like a fellow pilgrim whose beauty-loving soul bleeds in the face of the brutality perpetuated in the Americas, in the name of Christian freedom, since the day of Las Casas.

Lucien Richard and Barbara Darling-Smith address Christology. In "Christology and the Needs for Limits: Contextualization of Theology" Richard explores the question of the uniqueness of Christ. He adopts a "personal" model wherein the intentional self is not only the receiver of cultural constraints but is also a transformer of such constraints. While the concept of uniqueness is problematic for the historical method, the personal paradigm allows space for uniqueness in culture. From this perspective the "facticity" of history or experience remains ambiguous. The truth of Christology is above all a question of the concretion of personal and cultural existence. Richard concludes with an invitation to openness to the other, which is also an invitation to question what we take for granted in our limited world.

Barbara Darling-Smith presents "A Feminist Christological Exploration." Drawing upon the insights of feminists Rosemary Radford Ruether, Carter Heyward, and Sallie McFague, she explores affirmations of Jesus which harmonize with women's self-affirmations in response to the traditional devaluation of women by the church, which has confused the maleness of Jesus with its claim that Jesus of Nazareth plays a unique role in reconciling humanity to God.

The next cluster of papers deals with developments in Latin America and Africa. Paul Deats and Alice Hageman discuss the relationship between the Protestant churches and the Marxist regime in Cuba. They divide the history of the Protestant presence in Cuba into before and after the Revolution of 1959. Before the Revolution "Patriotic Protestantism" (1868–1898) marked a period of transition from Spanish rule to an increasing dependency on the United States (1898–1940) and the emergence of "Ecumenism and Self-Awareness" (1940–1959). Deats and Hageman describe three periods since 1959: "Church-State Mutual Distrust" (1959–1969), "Peaceful Coexistence" (1969–1980) and "Rapprochement" (1980–1986).

Jeanne Gallo deals with a critical issue in the study of the Latin American Basic Ecclesial Communities. Using Troeltsch's church/sect/mysticism typology she asks: "Is the Basic Ecclesial Community a new type of religious social organization that follows from the response of Christian faith in Latin America to the modern world or is it of the church, sect, or mysticism type?" She uses Troeltsch's threefold criterion—the content of Christology, ecclesiology, and social ethics—for the analysis of the movement.

Festus Asana discusses African Christianity. His chapter, "The Indigenization of the Christian Faith in Cameroon," deals especially with the penetration of Protestantism into his country in the heart of Africa. Asana describes his land, its varied cultures and history, with a few but colorful strokes and then focuses on the interaction of Protestant missionaries with the African universe of the Cameroons. In his treatment of African traditional religion Asana argues that what the missionaries introduced to Africa was not God but Christianity. Asana points out with great care the sacrificial self-giving of many missionaries in Cameroon, yet, their Western Christianity was destined to clash with the perceptions and interests of an autochthonous church. The second half of the paper deals with issues related to these perceptions and interests, the movement toward institutional autonomy, and the indigenization of worship still in process in the country.

Preston Williams and Orlando Costas represent the minority churches in the United States. In "The African-American Tradition and Martin Luther King, Jr.," Williams examines the work of Dr. King, especially in terms of his role in the Southern Christian Leadership Conference, in light of the transformational approach to contextualization of the faith developed by the African-American community.

Costas tells us another case of "Survival, Hope, and Liberation." His paper is an interpretation of Piri Thomas' spiritual pilgrimage in the context of the Hispanic church. Piri Thomas is a Black Puerto Rican, born and reared in New York, who got into trouble with the law (serving six years of a fifteen-year sentence) and then became a Pentecostal. Costas' case study is based on Thomas' own testimony in *Savior, Savior, Hold My Hand*. Costas quotes abundantly from Piri Thomas' own text. The English of the barrio cannot be "polished" without being raped and the content of Thomas' text cannot be "summarized," in many instances, without violation. At the end, Costas also offers his own reflection on Thomas' love-hate relationship to the church, and the role of the Hispanic church in the psychological, cultural, and social survival of its community, on the one hand, and its limitations, especially its tendency to spiritualize liberation, on the other.

In "Theological Education in the Urban Context," Douglas Hall sets an agenda for the training of urban ministers focused on the realities, needs, and possibilities of the city. Hall starts with a theology that sees Christianity as basically an urban phenomenon and then moves toward some specific aspects of city life and ministry. Central to his approach is a method of analysis of the complex dynamics and heterogeneity of the urban environment. Urban ministers, if they are to serve the real needs of the city, should be trained in cross-cultural interaction, social analysis, and in ways to be flexible and creative. Above all they need to learn the urban communities' own agendas.

Talata Reeves was asked to write a paper on "A Prophetic Reconception of God for our Time" for the concluding section of the consultation. Her paper draws on the resources of the prophetic tradition of the Hebrew scriptures, especially the message of Amos to the nation of Israel. She focuses on the concept of "the Day of Yahweh" in 5:18–20 and argues that a comparative study of texts where the expression appears reveals a range of meanings which include elements of judgment, battle, natural disorders, theophanies, the human role in that day, and the establishment of a new order. This hermeneutical key opens the doors to "all aspects of our society."

It should be quite clear by now that the papers collected in this annual volume represent a rainbow of theological perspectives, concerns, and methods. We think that nothing else would do justice to our context, for the Boston Theological Institute is an ecumenical cluster of theological institutions representing a wide range of theological traditions, cultures, and agendas. This collection is, therefore, a conversation about *one faith in many cultures.*

Notes

1. The question presupposes Max Weber's definition of rationalization and the Weberian thesis that Western culture (including religion) is rationalized.

2. He argues that in original Brahmanism there were no castes (*The Arian Witness*, Introduction), yet his appeal is directed to the "instructed persons of that time-honored community of Arian-Hindus" ("Christ the True Prajapathi," in *The Relation Between Christianity and Hinduism*).

References

Baago, Kaj. 1969. *Pioneers of Indigenous Christianity.* Bangalore and Madras: The Christian Institute for the Study of Religion and Society, and The Christian Literature Society.

Banerja, Krishna Mohun. 1875. *The Arian Witness: or Testimony of Arian Scriptures in Corroboration of Biblical History and the Rudiments of Christian Doctrine, including Dissertations on the Original Home and Early Adventures of Indo-Arians.* Calcutta.

———. 1880. *Two Essays as Supplement to the Arian Witness.* Calcutta.

———. 1892. *The Relation Between Christianity and Hinduism.* Madras: C.L.S.

Conn, Harvey. 1977. "Contextualization: Where Do We Begin?" in *Evangelicals and Liberation*, C. Armerding, ed. Nutley, NJ: Presbyterian and Reformed Pub. Co.

Geertz, Clifford. 1968. *Islam Observed.* New Haven: Yale University Press.

Kraft, Charles. 1979. *Christianity in Culture.* Maryknoll, NY: Orbis.

Lash, W. 1955. "Reflections on Indigenization," *The Indian Journal of Theology*, vol. 4, no. 2.

Ministry in Context. 1972. Bromley, Kent: Theological Education Fund.

Schreiter, Robert. 1979. *Constructing Local Theologies.* Maryknoll, NY: Orbis.

PART ONE

RAISING THE ISSUES

CHAPTER 1

Contextualization, Contextuality, and Contextualism

Max L. Stackhouse

It may be useful, at the outset of our deliberations together, to reflect on some critical features of our topic and on some of the perils which attend it. My comments will focus on two questions. First, what is implied, and what is excluded, when we speak of "contextualizing the faith"? And secondly, how do we know a "context" when we see one?

My reflections are based, for the most part, on three studies. For an Evangelical perspective, I draw on Charles H. Kraft's *Christianity in Culture: A Study in Dynamic Biblical Theologizing in Cross-Cultural Perspective* (1979), perhaps the most extensive and careful conservative study of contextualization that has ever been done. For a Catholic perspective, I draw on Robert J. Schreiter's *Constructing Local Theologies* (1985), a book which, like Kraft's, uses sociological, anthropological, and cultural-linguistic analysis to propose how Christianity might best become indigenized in local settings and, in the process, modify our understanding of what theology is all about in the first place.

But, as will become clear in the course of my remarks, I draw most directly from an ecumenically oriented Protestant study just nearing completion. Entitled *Apologia: Contextualization, Globalization, and Mission in Theological Education*, this study attempts to analyze major current discussions in terms of their theological and methodological presuppositions. It has involved research papers, dialogue, and interchange with an international research team. Major contributions come from Nantawan Boonprasat Lewis, a former Buddhist from Thailand; J. G. F. Collison, an Indian Christian working in a predominantly Hindu context; Lamin Sanneh, a former Muslim and presently a leading Christian scholar of the impact of missions on African national and cultural identity; Ilse von Loewenclau, an East German biblical scholar; Lee Harding, an Anglican who has pastored in rural America; and several members of the Andover Newton Theological School faculty with international and missiological concerns. My responsibility has been to draft the study, and to analyze the various perspectives in it from the standpoint of the implicit philosophical, theological and social presuppositions. It is especially with these resources in mind that I make my comments.

Contextualization

The first thing that needs to be said is that "contextualizing the faith" has been a part of the mission of the church from the beginning. If we take Pentecost, as reported in Acts 2 as the birthday of the church, we will have to note that the disciples were filled with the Holy Spirit and began to preach in such a way that "each one heard them speaking in his own language." The faith was being contextualized. This point is now confirmed in a different way by modern biblical scholarship: we now know from historico-critical studies that the various books of the New Testament address particular audiences in different settings and that the way they present the message of Jesus Christ is differently formulated so that it can be heard in terms of the concerns of the people addressed. These concerns are not only ones of language, but are social, economic, political, familial, and ideological in character. The scriptures are laden with quite specific, concrete references to status groups, leaders and followers, movements, trends, classes, and cultural environments. It is presumed throughout that the gospel, the faith, is pertinent to, and can indeed be contextualized in, each and every context it addresses, and that it will bring change to these settings.

It should be mentioned at least in passing that contextualization of the faith has taken place in the long traditions of the churches in the postbiblical period in at least four ways. First, the message of good news was again and again contextualized linguistically as the scriptures were translated again and again. I think here not only of the Septuagint and the Vulgate, but of the efforts of Wyclif, Luther, and hundreds of lesser known figures who have produced and who are still producing vernacular versions of scripture. As Lamin Sanneh has pointed out in our Association of Theological Schools research team, this tendency of Christianity to translate its most sacred writings into the languages of the peoples both contrasts with the attitude toward context of many other religions and presumes that enough of the valid knowledge of God is already present in the cultures Christianity encounters that words expressive of the gospel are already present. Only the massive efforts to translate Buddhist writings by the Makayana movement is comparable.

Secondly, at quite a different level, the doctrine of the incarnation suggests that the very reality of the only true and transcendent God took the risk of contextualization in a very human, very concrete, very contextual person. And this doctrine is paralleled by the notion that the church, as the body of Christ, is the incarnate presence of the living Christ, taking many shapes and forms in multiple contexts of the world.

Thirdly, the church over the ages, as it moved into the Greco-Roman world, north into Europe, east to the Slavic and Middle Eastern lands, and subsequently around the world, has contextualized the faith wherever it went, even if missionaries sometimes resisted indigenization and wanted to preserve the exact forms of confession and practice they brought with them. In the process, the church has bound peoples of an enormous variety of backgrounds into a common witness to a common vision of God's truth and justice as known in and through Jesus Christ.

And finally, the contextualization of the faith has always involved a vision of common humanity, one which, like Judaism and Islam, has, in some measure, overcome the rampant polytheism to which humanity seems to be inclined. It is the frequent temptation of us all to manufacture gods and images of God in our own image, and to pay obeisance to that which reinforces the sanctity of our own clan, our own interests, our own needs. Recall the ancient Greek aphorism: If donkeys had gods they would all bray; and if lions had gods they would all have manes. Against the tendency to generate polytheisms, Christianity has attempted to include particularities in a larger vision of truth and justice, one that overcomes and does not simply reify polytheism. One key implication of this for our topic is that all peoples and groups, in all contexts, stand under the same standards of truth and justice.

The reason for mentioning these several biblical, traditional, doctrinal matters involved in "contextualizing the faith" is to make us alert to the fact that we are in the company of the saints of the past when we turn to the future and call for contextualization. What they did, without having this specific word for it, is a model for what the contemporary church must do as we think about the global mission of the church today and tomorrow. But we should be clear about several matters that are not so clear today. All of the previous efforts to which I have pointed presume that there is something about the faith itself which is true and just and of universal importance, and that we can, in some measure, know what that is and bring it to new contexts. Indeed, all of these previous efforts believed that precisely because the Gospel contains key understandings of reality which are universally true and just it must be contextualized.

Contextuality

The ways of talking about what is universally true and just have varied. The church fathers utilized Greek and Roman philosophical concepts to speak of the gospel, and to show that the biblical message was not simply the confessional preference of another sect reflecting a local piety, but a way of grasping, both theoretically and practically, a vision of the metaphysico-moral nature of God's truth and justice, which the most universalistic philosophies of the day could not, on their own, quite grasp. Medieval Christians in the West struggled with the debates between the "realists" and the "nominalists," arguing that the most important claims of Christianity referred to spiritual and ethical realities, which could be known, debated, and affirmed even if, in the particular contexts of experiential life, they could not be confirmed empirically. And more recently, since the Enlightenment, a great number of efforts have been made to identify the "essence" of Christianity, and to distinguish this from the "accidents" of social, cultural, linguistic, and historical context.

All these efforts presume a distinction between what my colleague Gabriel Fackre calls the "textuality" of the Christian faith and the "contextuality" of the church and our particular understandings of the faith. All believe that, at some level, Christianity is based on universally valid claims about the truth and justice of God. "The Word" is not the same as the words of our understanding, but some human, contextually conditioned words serve as valid "texts" because they point to the Word which is transcontextual. The most important aspects of the faith are distinct from the temporary socio-historical conditions in which they appear, from the changing ideologies in which they are expressed, and from the incidental experiences which may be of great importance to our own variable spiritualities, but which are not necessarily an expression of God's truth and justice.

We know these debates, as they show up in such modern studies as those by Kraft and Schreiter, in terms of the images of "kernel" and "husk," "seed" and "soil," "content" and "form," "gospel" and "cultural accoutrements," or, in Paul's terms, "treasure" and "earthen vessel." All these views suggest that there is an ecumenical, catholic, orthodox, and context-invariant "core" of the Christian faith which can and must be distinguished from the contextual packages in which it is inevitably wrapped. Much has been written to show that again and again, biblical exegetes, missionaries, theologians, and ordinary believers, confuse the two and thus engage in one or another instance of idolatry or imperialism by taking highly relative social, political, economic, or cultural structures as part of the "essence."

Three recommended remedies have been proposed to deal with this. One is to insist that the church preach only the "pure gospel," with the understanding that it is like a seed which can be planted in various soils. As the plants and the flowers grow, it is presumed they will take on nutrients from the local environment, and eventually develop into an "indigenized" new version of the faith. A second approach is to use those modern critical sciences of historiography, sociology, anthropology, and comparative religious studies which accent a hermeneutic of suspicion to expose where contextual "vessels" have been confused with the gospel "treasure." The problem with these remedies is that they presume that it is possible to identify the "pure gospel" without social, political or cultural overtones, which is doubtful, or that we can strip away all the developments of tradition produced by centuries of interaction between the faith and its multiple contexts, which is unhistorical.

Still a third remedy has been proposed in our study team by Nantawan B. Lewis, drawing on the work of Letty Russell, Richard Schaul and several Asian theologians. She suggests that a decisive criterion for a Christian understanding of contextuality is whether or not it leads to intercontextual understandings of both the "texts" of the Christian faith and the interdependence of the contexts of the church. Only intercontextual views of contextuality could be a reflection of the transcontextual power of God present in each context.

In spite of such suggestions, however, many of the current understandings of contextuality have taken the "Feuerbachian step." That is, many continue to be so deeply influenced by nineteenth-century romantic and historicist thinking about these matters that they have begun to demand acknowledgment of the "contextual" character of the "text"—of the core, the kernel, the treasure, itself. Feuerbach, you will remember, argued in 1841 that the "essence of Christianity," and indeed of all religions, is a projection of context-derived interests, needs, hopes, and dreams onto a cosmic screen. His argument is paralleled in different forms by Marx, Neitzsche, Freud, Mannheim, and a host of modern scholars, who protect "idealism" and claim that there is no identifiable core, kernel, text, essence, treasure or gospel other than what specific groups project on the world as a reflection of their own context. If we want to know what people mean when they speak of these things, we do not examine their claims in terms of their possible transcontextual truth or justice or intercontextual significance, we examine them in terms of the immediate contextual forces which have generated them. These are the roots of the modern, contextualist "hermeneutics of suspicion."

It is all well and good for Evangelicals such as Kraft to want to separate "the biblical message" from the contextual biases of missionaries so that it can become more easily contextualized among the peoples of the world. But for any who have taken the Feuerbachian step, there is a profound suspicion that they can identify any "biblical message," because the parts of the Bible derive from different contexts. And it is all well and good for Catholics such as Schreiter to want to distinguish those aspects of church doctrine which are the product of Western "local theologies" from the truly catholic doctrines which express perennial dimensions of the power of the Holy Spirit, so that these truly catholic dogmas may be woven into the fabric of new local theologies. But whether any doctrines are or could be truly catholic is precisely what is under intense debate today.

Such scholars as these have made major contributions insofar as they have put on firm theoretical grounds what every pastor, missionary, participant in interfaith dialogue, and believer already knows: we must learn how to listen to contexts discerningly and learn how to recognize the contextuality of most of what we humans say even when we think we are contextualizing the "eternal truths" of the gospel. Their efforts are fully in accord with the theological doctrine of sin, which, among other things, reminds us of the pretense involved if we think we can "have" the pure truth of God or that we can "do" the justice of God without ambiguity. Their efforts also accord with theological doctrines of providence in that they demand recognition that many social and cultural systems can see the means by which God cares for people. But they may not yet have recognized how some interpretations of contextuality undercut the possibilities of contextualizing the faith precisely because some of the tools of contextual analysis methodologically deny that the faith is any different from, or more than, the context from which it derives.

Contextualism

Among those who have absolutized the tools of contextual analysis, one can also find an understanding of contextuality which approximates an ideology sufficiently that we can call it "contextualism." It appears, currently, in those versions of liberation theology which take one model of contextual analysis, based on the master-slave relationship, and the movement of history to revolution, as the key to all problems of faith and context, truth and justice. I do not want to be misunderstood on this point, and hence I want to affirm at the outset of my remarks on liberation thought that I believe that no Christian can fail to approve efforts to overcome tyranny and exploitation which have plagued colonialized peoples, women, and minorities in this country. As a matter of justice, we must make a preferential option for the poor and the oppressed. Nor can we deny that at least some causes of poverty and oppression have been legitimated by one or another construal of Christianity at the hands of white, male, capitalist Northern Europeans who have confused their material interests with the gospel and tried to make everyone else do the same. Many of those committed to liberation are aiding the justice of God when they point out such contextual perversions of the gospel as sinful.

But it can be asked of those who have pointed out the contextuality of this pathology whether or not their valid insights are not also sometimes freighted with a more dubious "contextualism" that may distort our understandings of the truth and justice of God. By this I mean the dogmatic denial that anything universally true exists, and that everything of basic significance grows out of the contextual experience of those on the underside of master-slave relationships. It is frequently implied by some committed to a liberationist approach to theology and ethics that truth emerges from the actual material needs and interests of oppressed peoples, and only from that source. Often this claim is linked to a denial of the validity of any loyalty to, or talk about, universals, essences, metaphysical or moral principles, and the like. Indeed, such ways of talking are seen to be the product of some false "dualism" between text and context, theory and practice, or faith and life, reflecting the alienated consciousness of Western philosophy, theology, and "abstract" ethics.

The difficulties which contextualism poses are of several kinds, most of them having to do with questions of "truth," which, if not adequately answered, will discredit and finally undercut the drive for justice. First, if the contextualism is taken as our central way of working, we cannot speak of "contextualizing the faith," for there would be no "faith" distinct from what is already in the context to contextualize. We could speak only of "expressing" the various faiths of various contexts. And the only way of validating any particular expression of faith would be to ascertain whether it accurately reflects the interests of those on the bottom edge of society. Secondly, nothing could be "globalized" without imperialism, for every attempt at globalization would be nothing but the imposition of what emerges from one context onto other contexts. And thirdly, many who take contextualism as a way of working do so as Christians and appeal to the Bible or to the great catholic teachings of the Christian tradition—such as the doctrines of the Trinity, the offices of Christ, or the importance of the Sacraments—to legitimate their efforts. But it is probably dishonest to claim that the Bible, the great doctrines, and sacramental practices developed out of the concerns which the advocates of contextualism see as decisive for understanding the human condition.

And finally, contextualism implies that only those in a specific context can speak about it meaningfully. All others must remain silent, especially if they are in any way critical of what is going on or of what people say to be true or just in that context. The worst thing that could happen would be to attempt to convert a people in a particular context to another point of view. A privileged epistemological status is accorded to specific peoples in specific contexts. This privileged status can take one of two forms: a "hard" absolutist one or a "soft" relativist one. In its absolutist form, contextualism becomes an inverted dogmatism: "We, because we are in this context, know something that no one on the outside can know, and anyone who does not accept our version of truth and justice is to be, at least, excommunicated or, at most, doomed to destruction." In its relativist form, contextualism claims that what we say, from our context, is valid for us, even if others cannot understand what we are talking about. It is surely true that all must listen to the voices of those in particular contexts most attentively to try to hear what they are talking about, especially if they have been denied a voice in common discourse. But both of these, in fact, deny the possibilities of common discourse, of dialogue, and of the attempt to discern what is true in all human contexts, whether we are directly a part of them or not.

It is doubtful whether only people in a particular context can understand what is true or false, what is just or unjust, in that context, or that others must take what they say in that specific context as the indisputable truth. The twentieth century struggle to articulate universal human rights, valid for Uganda, Kampuchea, Afghanistan, South Africa, and Chile, whether or not the people know them, express them, or find their interests served by them, is one way of speaking of truth and justice beyond any epistemological privilege. Contextualism is interested in human rights only when they serve the material interests of a preferred group. Still another way is to wrestle globally, even cosmically, with the findings of modern natural scientists, which put all our localistic battles into the perspective of "creation" and its transcontextual significance, as, for example, Roger Shinn and James Gustafson have done. Contextualism sees such perspectives as too global. Further, if it is true that only those who are directly involved in a specific context can know what it means, then it would have to be admitted that only white, male, rich, Northern

Europeans could say anything about the dominant theological traditions, and all others would have to remain silent. These implications are unconscionable.

In the final analysis the tendency of contextualism to deny that the truth of the gospel is not and cannot be something that is either transcontextual or intercontextual, tends also to corrupt justice. Contextualism is unable to bridge our divisions of race, class, sex, culture, and history. It can break down domination, but it cannot construct new visions of truth and justice, for these are seen as matters entirely relative to the race, class, sex, culture or history of a context. Soft contextualism is today the new form of polytheism; hard contextualism is the new fundamentalism of the left.

Today's contextualisms sharply challenge contemporary theology, ethics, and missiology. The possibility of the contextualization of the faith is threatened by the ways of understanding the contextuality of faith that become contextualism. I suggest that we be alert to the ambiguities of our uses of "contextuality," and that we attempt again to identify, articulate, examine, and, should we find it proper to do so, attempt to develop an apologia for the faith that we want to contextualize. It is not an easy task, for many modern ways of speaking about truth and justice, and indeed of God, are doubtful, even contemptuous, of the notion that "the faith" or the gospel refers to anything which could be transcontextual, and thus could and should be contextualized around the globe.

Context

At the outset of this presentation, I noted that my remarks would focus on two questions. I turn now, in this briefer part, to the second one: How do we know a context when we see one? If the first question led us into some philosophical and theological issues about the nature of the faith which we want to contextualize, this second question will lead us into some issues in social theory and philosophy of history as they bear on context. For whether we are going to contextualize the faith, or try to understand the contextual nature of our faith, we shall have to know what a context is. Let me put the question this way: How big is a context? How long does it last? Who is in it and who is out of it, and how do we know?

In one sense, this is a problem already faced by modern Christian ethics when it wrestled with "situation ethics." What is a "situation"? It turned out that when situation ethicists found themselves confronted with this question, they either could not answer or answered with such divergent responses that no one knew what the answer meant. Sometimes they meant a pastoral "case" which involved a conflict of values; sometimes they meant a dilemma of conscience; sometimes they meant a "problem" to which all solutions seemed to produce bad consequences, and sometimes they meant a crisis where it seemed necessary to do something wrong (such as use violence) to stop a great evil (such as that represented by Hitler).

Similar confusion seems to attend even the best treatments of contextualization and contextuality. We are interested in contextualizing the faith and in contextuality because we think that the gospel has something to say "here and now." But how big is a "here" and how long is a "now"? Frequently, we hear phrases like "in the Latin American context," or "in the Asian context," but it does not take very much listening to these contexts to learn that the context of Nicaragua is different from the context of Brazil in Latin America, or that the context of the Philippines is different from the context of India in Asia. And, indeed, in Brazil, the context of Sao Paulo differs from the context of the upper Amazon, and in India, the context of Kerala differs from that of the Punjab. And in both Brazil and India the context of the landless peasant differs from that of the tribal and of the industrial worker and of the university student. We are forced to ask what it is that defines the boundaries of a context: regionality, nationality, cultural-linguistic history, ethnicity, political system, economic class, gender identity, social status, or what? Contemporary social theorists and social ethicists have developed a number of terms to attempt to identify the decisive meanings of "context." Phenomenological thinkers, such as Gibson Winter, have attempted to speak of context in terms of the "life-world" in which people find their identity. Contextual ethicists, such as Paul Lehmann, speak often of the *koinonia*, or "community." Anthropologists speak of "cultures"; sociologists of "societies" or "social systems"; and those doing comparative studies speak of "civilizations." The problem is that each of these definitions entails a different way of understanding the decisive contours of human contexts, of what the "here" is to which contextual thinking wants to draw our attention.

In the same breath, we have to ask about the historical duration of a context, since every known context is changing. Shall we define the "now" of Latin America in terms of the deep heritage of Iberian colonialism encountering indigenous cultures, as Prof. Fuentes of Harvard does? Perhaps we should focus on the history of American interventions since the Spanish-American War and the development of multinational capitalist interests simultaneously with the doctrine of "manifest destiny" at the turn of the twentieth century. Or shall we heed the political rhetoric of our day and define the Latin American context in terms of the post–World War II confrontations between communism and democracy, as the debates over funding the "contras" do? More personally, perhaps we should give special attention to those in sanctuary who tell of their family situations in the last decade. What, in brief, is the time-frame of our understanding of a context?

Again, social ethicists draw much from social historians who provide definitions of "periodization"—that is, of why and how the study of the past can and should be broken into time units so that we can know the difference between the dominant institutions, structures, and ideas of historical epochs. We have come to speak, conventionally, of the "medieval period," the "age of reform" and the "age of reason," and the present (sometimes called the "modern age," sometimes called the "post modern age"). But when we turn to the contexts of, say, Asia and Africa, this periodization makes much less sense. All the problems I have already noted in regard to the breadth and width of any "here" reappear in regard to the definitions of the length of a "now." What is it that makes a contextual period a time unit? Is it the level of technology, the nature of governance, the predominant structures of law, the relationship of the classes or of the sexes or of the generations, the level of artistic creativity, or what? If we use any of these indicators in describing what is the temporal boundary of a context, we have made a judgment about what we believe really drives human history, and thus is to be taken as the measure of significant contextual discernment.

The reason these tools of analysis have been developed is that contexts do not define themselves. A socio-historical hermeneutic is required, and one of the most perplexing issues of our day is the question of which tools of social and historical analysis both reveal the deepest meanings of a context and open it to the possibility of contextualizing the faith.

Some seem to think that it would be a wonderful thing if we could but take one or another of these social scientific concepts, link it with a clear periodization, and say "that is what we mean when we use the word 'context.' " And that, in fact, is what many of us do when we speak of a "context"—our own or someone else's. Sadly, things are not so easy, for every choice that we make in these areas is freighted with lopsided interpretations of contextuality, and some choices lead inevitably to contextualism. And even if we found some way of combining all these sciences and interpretive periodizations in a "unified" theory, it is not certain that we would "know" any context exhaustively. That is because every context is a particular manifestation of the human condition, which cannot be understood without reference to God, God's laws, God's purpose, and God's love, which transcends every context and every social hermeneutic.

It may be that the best we can do is simply make it clear to one another that when we say the word "context," we are using it provisionally. We are looking at some socio-cultural situation from an angle that involves any number of limitations. Thus, we could study—for example, as Rubem Alves has recently done in *Protestantism and Repression*, the context of urban Brazil in the post-World War II period and looked at it in terms of the complicity of Evangelicalism in morally legitimizing some features of political and economic domination. If we do that, we recognize that others may look at the religious, demographic, social, and cultural context in Brazil in a much longer period of time and come to different conclusions about the context. The test would be whether our particular ways of construing our contexts are open to intercontextual and transcontextual realities.

This raises the prospect of still another, better possibility, one implied in the title of our consultation. Perhaps it is possible to think that we are still in the age of contextualizing the faith, an age which extends from Pentecost to the eschaton, and a faith that is relevant to every particular context. If that is so, we will see our encounters with and analyses of life-worlds, of societies, cultures and civilizations as but episodes in the global mission of the church. If that is so, we would be called, above all, to understand the perils of any contextuality which does not reach toward intercontextual and transcontextual possibilities. If that is so, Wesley had it right when he said "the world is my parish," and Troeltsch had it right when he wrote "history is our epoch." These are the contexts for the gospel.

CHAPTER 2

A Critical Contextual Approach to the Social Function of Religions: Mission, Imperialism, and Accomplishment

Jane Cary Peck

A critical contextual approach to the social function of religion involves study of purposes and effects of contextualizing the faith. In Latin America Christians are present on all sides of revolutionary struggles, which leads me to examine and evaluate different social functions of religion in different and the same contexts. This examination involves analysis of influences of, at least, history, social location, and politico-economic interests, theology, and praxis. The focus chosen for this study is the Central American context where revolutionary struggles are particularly vigorous today, a context which varies widely from a nonrevolutionary situation of historically democratic Costa Rica, through liberation struggles in El Salvador and Guatemala, and the United States militarization of Honduras, to the revolutionary situation of Nicaragua's national reconstruction and struggle against the United States-backed counterrevolutionary war.

I take as background assumptions of this paper several points from Otto Maduro's work, *Religion and Social Conflicts* (1982):

1. Marxist theory of religion as a societal product does not exhaust the reality of religion. True, religion is a situated reality, specific context, and historical moment. And the structure of society limits and orients the possibilities for action and any religion within it: religious activity is limited and oriented by its social context. But religion is not merely a product of social relationships. It is also a relatively autonomous microsocial network with a degree of reality and stability of its own: it is a relatively autonomous producer of social relationships. Society acts on religion, and religion acts on itself.

14

2. Further, religion acts on society and social conflicts; it influences society and social struggles. Here there is a dual potential: a conservative function, which reinforces the power of the dominating class, and a revolutionary function.

Conservative Function

Marxists and many others have criticized the "cultural captivity of the church." As Maduro, argues, dominant classes have both the interest and material means to place religion at the service of the extension and consolidation of the dominance exercised by these same classes. Also it is characteristic of churches, as Troeltsch maintained, to become accommodated to their culture, perceive a vested interest in preserving and extending the culture, and thereby forfeit their capacity for prophetic witness in the culture on behalf of the poor. Contemporary ecumenical ethics has criticized Western churches for their cultural captivity in more specific terms, as generally part of and supportive of the politico-economic status quo, identifying with and collaborating with the dominant social forces and structures in society.

This is especially borne out in the Latin American church, child of Western Roman Catholic and Protestant missionary parents. The history of the Latin American church is the history of cross and crown arriving simultaneously in the colonial conquest of Latin America, the cross serving the crown's conquest; Protestant missionaries entered at the invitation of liberal national aristocracies in the service of the neocolonial project of modernization over against Catholic rigidity and cultural control. The missionaries were, as Ruy Costa notes (Costa, 1985) emissaries of the elites: the national aristocracies that invited them and the foreign elites that selected them and controlled mission policy. They performed a social function of support for the establishment, serving the interests of the dominant domestic business-military elite aligned with an international political-economic-military elite—namely interests in cheap, skilled labor, markets, and raw materials. José Míguez Bonino writes: "Protestantism, in terms of its historical origin, its introduction to Latin America, and its ethos, came into our world as the religious accompaniment of free enterprise liberal capitalist democracy" (Míguez, 12). As the child primarily of North American Protestantism, Latin American Protestantism subscribes to ideologies which postulate a harmony of interests between the developed capitalist countries of the Northern hemisphere and the nations of the Southern. But this interdependence is imbalanced toward one pole, and therefore, Latin American Protestantism strengthens the dependence—economic, cultural, ideological, and religious—of Latin America in relation to the capitalist world. The church is thereby an agent of dependence, legitimating First World interests in the Third World. Its social function is legitimation of the established order: external North American economic domination of Latin America (with political import) in collaboration with domestic economic and military elites.

The masses of the people have not benefited but suffered under liberalism's modernizing project: its achievements have been the privilege of the elite. Religion has not only nurtured morally upright, hard workers for the economic system, but has mollified some of those suffering under the system. Repressive police states have also been necessary to protect the system. Churches have thus been ideological allies of foreign and national elites keeping Latin America in dependence and the masses of the people in need and even oppression.

Today the Protestant church in Latin America is to be found largely on the side of the dominant military and economic elites (with notable exceptions). It has not protested the establishment of authoritarian and absolute states (usually military dictatorships), incapacitation of judicial power, intimidation of legislatures, censorship, or violation of human rights. Instead, it has assumed attitudes of silence, sometimes approval, and even cooperation with the dominant order, so that, in contrast with the Roman Catholic Church, Protestant churches up until recently have suffered little state pressure.

The primary factors which contribute to this conservative social function are Protestantism's dependence, theology, authoritarianism, and ideology.

Dependence

There is a linkage between Latin American economic and cultural dependence and its Protestant religious dependence. Latin American Protestantism, as a child, even an extension, of North American Protestantism, has been dependent for its leadership and resources on North American mission agencies. It draws from North American theology a pietistic, spiritualistic, individualistic theology and an ideology of "manifest destiny." All of this supports the modernist project of free enterprise economic development of Latin America.

This is graphically illustrated in the case of Costa Rica in a study by Robert Craig (Craig, 1981) and my own research (1984). Seventy-two percent of Protestant churches in Costa Rica have their headquarters in the United States. Costa Rican churches are dependent on the United States for religious media programing and audiovisual and print materials: the 700 Club and PTL Club are broadcast on several channels and United States religious radio programs are used. Five of the six religious publishers in Costa Rica are North American (the sixth is Spanish). Sunday school curricula are published in the United States. The 700 Club regularly broadcasts explicit religious right political issues. Its overall theme is that the United States has a divine mission: it has been elected by God to guide and save the world. Craig concludes that Costa Rican Protestantism is "a case of dependency" whose ideology and theology function to support the status quo and to undercut liberation. Its religious message is a product of the bourgeois North American world, and its sociopolitical impact is not only the perpetuation of domination and legitimation of the established order, but also the perpetuation of an ideology whose consequences are a false understanding of the structural nature of oppression, dependence on the North American world, and a faith that obstructs the possibility of liberation.

Pietism

Based on pietistic theological positions that are conservative and antiworld, with a radical dichotomy between the spiritual and the material/worldly, conservative missionaries and Central American mission churches reject political action for Christians. The earth is seen as a waiting room for life eternal. The arena for Christian mission is the individual and spiritual realms, avoiding the lower and distracting material realm, toward the end of personal salvation of souls through individual reconciliation with God. The moral world of conservative evangelical missionaries and receiving Central American churches is personal, not social; spiritual life is individual life in relation with God. Religion thus tends to be blind to injustice and contradictions in social life, thereby supporting the status quo. In their eschatology, the Kingdom of God is radically separate from human history, all is in God's hands, and therefore no human action toward the Kingdom is necessary or possible, and we should be subject to established political authority. Theological pietism often appears even among missionaries sent by liberal mainline denominations such as the United Methodist.

Authoritarianism

Central American Protestantism curtails autonomy and critical thought by sanctions of exclusion and schism in cases of theological differences. There have been recent examples of this phenomenon in Costa Rica in the case of professors of theology. Strong reliance on the authority of the state is an important manifestation of Protestantism's authoritarianism.

Ideological Anti-Ideology

Despite a strong anti-ideological stance in an assertion of the transcendence of faith over ideologies, missionaries and Central American churches espouse an explicit anticommunist "national security" ideology and an ideology of "manifest destiny." The fight against subversive, godless communism is a primary Christian cause and justifies church support of Latin American governments, their repressive measures, and United States military aid. Christian governments have a manifest destiny to protect Christian civilization. Communism is the primary enemy of the church, but the church is unable to combat the enemy alone; help is available from collaboration with the national power which has the same primary enemy. (Note that these Christians are dependent on political authority to withstand enemies of the faith.)

From these religious beliefs ensues the conservative social function of the missionary church. These Protestant churches favor the status quo in the liberation struggles of the continent. This is especially so of sects and independent Protestant churches, not so of interdenominational Protestant organizations and a few local churches.

Illustrations of Sectarian Propagation

In Central America in general, there are several categories of non-Catholic religious groups: the historical, mainline denominations, Pentecostal churches, pseudo-Christian sects, non-Christian sects (Unification Church), and service institutions. The majority of Pentecostals are traditionally spiritualistic and fundamentalist. But there is also a strong tendency toward political and ideological radicalization against popular movements in Central America, especially in new sects directed from the United States and financed from outside, marked by anticommunist militancy and counterinsurgency plans. (A typical case is the Iglesia del Vervo in Guatemala, known for its prophet, the former dictator General Ríos Montt.) New sects are arriving in San Salvador from the United States. One priest commented that on Sundays in his parish in a poor *barrio* in San Salvador, there was at least one sect activist for every ten families. Both pseudo-Christian and non-Christian sects actively campaign against communism and liberation theology and aggressively proselytize.

In Nicaragua new sects have proliferated in the years since the triumph of the revolution. Found along border zones in conflict between Nicaragua and Honduras, in areas of large indigenous population, and in refugee camps, they have been used to "soften" *campesinos* for counterrevolution. The counterrevolutionary function of religion in Nicaragua is both covert and overt. Some sect leaders preach against participation in the cotton and coffee harvests and the military draft, and help youth leave the country to evade military conscription. They give religious sanction to middle-class demands: "No one can be Christian without private property"; "Cooperative farms are unchristian." Storefront sects have not only refused to use their facilities for neighborhood inoculation programs and continuing literacy training but have played their expensive, huge loudspeakers at top volume during evening adult education classes in the neighborhood. They denounce Christian participation in the militia and army (although there is no religious tradition of conscientious objection in Nicaragua) and Christian political activity, especially priests in government. These groups, along with some of the Roman Catholic hierarchy, are in close contact with the United States embassy, North American religious groups which raise large sums of money for the "contras" (such as the Christian Broadcast Network), and with "contra" leaders.

This religion serves the interests of the former elite and United States financial and political interests. Its anti-ideological national security doctrine supports the policies of the United States and Salvadoran governments. This counterrevolutionary social function of religion in Nicaragua is contributing to the destabilization and even overthrow of the government. It is a new project of conquest, aligned with the North American religious right in its anticommunism and private fund-raising for the "contras"; a reactionary project of change back to domination by the United States and the privileged United States-oriented domestic elite.

A Church of God pastor, Rodolfo Fonseca, makes rejoinder to the antipolitical preaching of conservative Nicaraguan religion, harking back to the missionary legacy and its social function and leading us to discussion of a different social function of religion:

> So how are we Christians to be preaching only the spiritual gospel, leaving to the so-called Marxists and atheists what we are supposed to be doing? That spiritualized Christianity is what our missionaries with blue eyes and beautiful hair and a fragrance of heaven taught us. If we preach only that . . . then those who are helping the poor show themselves to be more Christian than we who claim to be Christians.
>
> So the context we live in obliges us to reflect and go back to the Bible and reread it . . . [Fonseca, 1983].

Accompaniment

Otto Maduro's work on the function of religion in society demonstrates the changing role of religion depending on its worldview and its class links. He maintains that in acting on society, religion has a dual potential: the conservative function I have been discussing, or a revolutionary function—delegitimizing the status quo and fostering the construction of a new society. Let me turn now to this second alternative, the revolutionary function, or what I am calling a mission of accompaniment.

Maduro concludes that religion can be an intervening variable in a class struggle for greater autonomy from oppression, if the religious role-players work together with members of oppressed classes to achieve their autonomy from the culture and psychic control of the worldview of the controlling classes.

Social Location

From a starting point of pastoral activity with the poor and nonpersons, first Roman Catholic and now many Protestant missioners and churches in Central America have begun to live out a different Christian mission and perform a different, even revolutionary, social function. Tomás Borge of Nicaragua and José Míguez Bonino of Argentina, among others, contribute to my understanding of this reality. Borge accounts for the exceptional Christian participation in the Nicaraguan revolution as partly related to the Nicaraguan church tradition of being close to the people (peasants and workers), unlike other historical examples in which the church was divorced from the poor. This contact with the people and their pain, the poverty of the masses, the repression by the enemy, and the participation of many priests who were revolutionary and identified with the interests of the people gave Nicaraguan Christianity a very active participation in the revolutionary process (Borge, 1981).

Míguez adds a theoretical and intentional dimension to this insight as he addresses social location, an important aspect of contextualization (Míguez, 43–44). Social location is not only a matter of fate or circumstance, but also of option and decision. Though we are situated in reality, we can also position ourselves differently in relation to that situation. The ethical question therefore passes through the decision about one's own social position, option, goal of one's work, and the like. On the basis of an eschatological ethics of justice, the church in mission may assume solidarity with the poor as its specific commitment, may explicitly opt for such a loyalty, do its work with and in behalf of the poor, accompany them on their way, walk with them. As John C. Bennett says, we discover God's will partly through understanding the needs of God's people (Bennett, 8). With a method and option of starting with the reality of the poor, the church sees God's will differently and becomes different in the process of responding. Its mission and social function are changed.

A Liberating Current in Protestantism

Pablo Richard sees historical, mainline Protestant denominations in Central America (Episcopalian, Baptist, Methodist, Presbyterian, Moravian, Mennonite) as beginning to be "pierced by a renovating and liberating current" (Richard, 1985). These churches are characterized by a liberation current formed by minority groups within, which have supported the ecumenical movement in the region. Two Protestant seminaries, Seminario Bíblico in Costa Rica and Seminario Bautista in Nicaragua, as well as several ecumenical theological research centers, are also marked by this liberating current.

Further, an opposite tendency to the one I spoke of earlier can be seen in the Pentecostal churches, the most numerous non-Roman Catholic religious group. This is an impulse toward an ecclesiastical institutionalization, an ecumenical opening with the historical churches, and a current of liberation theology. (A well-known example is the Iglesia Pentecostal Fe y Santidad of Cartago, Costa Rica, and Richard cites others in Guatemala.) Protestant pastors and missionaries have been martyred, imprisoned, or expelled from certain Central American countries because of their revolutionary commitment to the gospel and their radical commitment to the poor.

Praxis of Accompaniment

The mission of accompaniment which performs a revolutionary rather than conservative social function in Central America is a praxis of ministry with a chosen social location and a theological starting point: *el pueblo de los pobres*—the people, the poor masses; a project of communion—standing with the people, and even more, walking with, accompanying the people on their way, in their struggles.

There are many expressions of this accompaniment in Protestant churches and mission:

preaching
organizing churches
teaching in seminaries
medical practice
work education and literacy
   training
rehabilitation work with
   former prostitutes and criminal
   offenders
forestry work

music and poetry
agricultural reform
"pastorale of women"
Christian base communities
ministry in war zones,
   new settlements, and
   refugee camps
theological publications
   and continuing
   theological education

theological reflection, research, training
grassroots pastoral agents—through the Centro Valdivieso
   and Instituto Histórico documentation projects and
   publications—conferences on Christian faith and
   revolution, projects of relating faith to context
working with Nicaraguans in CEPAD (Evangelical Committee
   for Aid and Development) on arguments
   to the government for conscientious objection;
investigating possible human rights abuses,
reports to U.S. mission boards and denominations, publications, communications to the U.S. government,
   working ecumenically,
   and more

This is the mission of accompaniment in the church called *la iglesia que nace del pueblo*—the church being born from the people. Affirming the gospel as God's good news to the poor, it has given voice to the voiceless poor in their cry to God from their oppression and nobodiness; it is denouncing political and military repression and economic oppression in Central America; it is analyzing forms of oppression, linkages, and root causes; it has moved from a bourgeois orientation to a class option for the poor; and it is walking beside the poor as they struggle for their liberation. This church is also announcing the good news: that God is with the poor, incarnate as one of them, harkening to their cries, and leading them out of their oppression. In the mission of accompaniment, the church is proclaiming God's commonwealth from among the poor and oppressed, following the example of Christ.

Fruits of Liberating Faith

The fruits of accompaniment among the oppressed class are a changing worldview in and through theology, political analysis, literacy, economic empowerment, renewal of indigenous culture, and development of class consciousness and mobilization. There is also a contextualization of missionaries' faith (in terms of the influence of the host environment on the incoming faith): missionaries and churches are becoming evangelized by the poor, experiencing evangelical renewal, gleaning faith to evangelize U.S. churches and Christians. The mission of accompaniment is changing the shape of mission; it is a qualitative change toward liberation, life, and profound spiritual renewal.

This tendency in some Protestant, as well as Catholic churches and missionaries, is a manifestation of the potential Maduro sees for religion to perform a revolutionary social function, to aid in the autonomous development of subordinated classes and the reinforcement of their alliances against domination. In the religious mission of accompaniment, liberating grace enables the poor to become the subjects of their lives, and provides, for religion and the church, evangelical renewal.

References

Bennett, John C. 1975. *The Radical Imperative*. Philadelphia: Westminster.

Borge, Tomás. 1981. Mimeographed interview circulated in Nicaragua, Spring 1981.

Costa, Ruy. "Contextualization: A Quest for Communion or Conquest? A Look at the Protestant Presence in Latin America" (unpublished paper presented to the First Colloquium of Third World Scholars, Aug. 1, 1985).

Craig, Robert. "El papel y funcion de las Iglesias Protestantes en la vida costaricanse: Un caso de dependencia" (unpublished: April 1981).

Fonseca, Rodolfo. "A Discussion of Salvation," *Sojourners*, March 1983.

Maduro, Otto. 1982. *Religion and Social Conflicts*. Maryknoll, NY: Orbis.

Míguez Bonino, José. 1983. *Toward a Christian Political Ethics*. Philadelphia: Fortress.

Peck, Jane Cary. "Reflections from Costa Rica on Protestantism's Dependence and Nonliberative Social Function," *Journal of Ecumenical Studies*, Spring, 1984.

Richard, Pablo. "El Salvador: A Church that Accompanies the People." San Salvador: Fe y Práctica, June 1985.

PART TWO

HISTORICAL PERSPECTIVES

CHAPTER 3

Christ as the Divine Guru in the Theology of Roberto de Nobili

Francis X. Clooney

The State of the Question

Roberto de Nobili was born in 1577 in Rome, became a Jesuit in 1596, and lived in Madurai in South India from 1606 until a few years before his death in 1656 (in Mylapore). In sharp contrast with most of the earlier Portuguese missionaries working out of Goa, he attempted to present the gospel in a form less foreign to the Hindus among whom he worked. He first described himself as a European of the second "noble" or *kṣatriya* caste, and later became a renunciant (*sannyāsī*) dressing like a Hindu holy man. He learned the local languages—Sanskrit, Tamil and Telegu— fluently, long before any other European gained comparable proficiency. As a result of this effort, it became possible for Hindus to see conversion to Christianity as a spiritual possibility (whether or not they actually took up the challenge) rather than a political/economic maneuver. De Nobili insisted that those who did convert be allowed to maintain most of the external forms of their previous way of life, and not to start dressing, eating, and so forth, like the Portuguese.

De Nobili has rightly been held up as one of the best early examples of cultural adaptation in evangelization (Cronin, 1959; Rajamanickam, 1972). Yet the impression given—accentuated by his controversies with Goa and then Rome over issues of appearance, such as whether Brahmin converts could continue to live and dress as Brahmins—has been that his work was only a matter of appearances: the presentation of the clear and unchanging truth enunciated in the Counter-Reformation Roman Church in "garb"—words and images acceptable to Hindus.

This view is to some extent supported by the tone of de Nobili's own writings, which are quite often controversial and apologetic, as he criticizes a variety of

Hindu viewpoints, particularly doctrines such as *avatāra* (periodic divine descents into the world) and rebirth. Again and again, as for instance in his great fundamental work, the *Āttuma Nirnaya* (*Treatise on the Soul*), he argues from certain principles of reason (which he assumes are available to all humans) to the truth of specific Catholic doctrines. One may conjecture that his desire to present the gospel in Indian terms may not have included a (much more modern) awareness that concepts and words are themselves "cultural garb" in need of adaptation.[1] Modern hermeneutical problems did not arise in any explicit fashion for de Nobili.

But if his work functioned simply at this level of adaptation in cultural externals, along with the presentation of an unchanging truth, his example would be inadequate for us who have been made sensitive to the cultural relativity of the thoughts and words in which we express doctrines. We are all to some extent uneasy with an idea of inculturation that presumes a body of knowledge, however sacred, merely "packaged" differently in different cultures. Modern sensitivities about the so-called European domination of theology and about the need for "Third World theologies" challenge us to go much further than de Nobili might seem to have gone if he did stop at "externals."

Even regarding de Nobili himself, a more immediate question can be asked: Is it likely that someone could live for fifty years in a Hindu environment, eat and live and dress like a Hindu, learn Hindu scriptures and philosophy, internalize Hindu dialectics sufficiently so as to argue adeptly with Hindus— without interiorizing and "owning" some of that religion and religious truth?

It is the thesis of this presentation that de Nobili's Indian experience *did* color his understanding of the Christian faith itself. I will argue that he understood the religious options available in the Hinduism of his time sufficiently that he could make an apt choice for his presentation of Christ: *Christ was the divine guru come down on earth.* This choice made the Christian teaching more attractive to his Hindu audience, and yet distanced it from the more obvious parallel with the Incarnation, the *avatāra* theory of divine descents into the world. Secondly, and of equal importance, I will argue that *this contextualization potentially sheds new light on the meaning of the Incarnation itself*, since the Indian idea of the guru is spiritual in a way different from and probably richer than the European notion of the "teacher." In the third and final section of this essay I will draw some more general conclusions from this historical instance for our own general theory of inculturation or contextualization.[2]

God as the Divine Teacher (divya guru)

De Nobili's exposition of the purpose of the Incarnation constitutes a major portion (chap. 6–12) of his great apologetic work, the *Dūṣaṇa Tikkāram* ("Refutation of calumnies"), to which my analysis of de Nobili's thought is here limited. His concern is to establish the rational plausibility of divine embodiment in human flesh, without rationalizing it as simply another case of *avatāra*, divine descents in human (or animal) form.[3] Three points elaborated particularly in his chapter 8 warrant our attention: (1) the description of the human condition such as requires the incarnation; (2) the purpose of God in undertaking it; (3) the conditions "imposed" on God in enacting it.[4]

The Human Condition

De Nobili describes the human condition (*saṁsāra*; [de Nobili, 1964:8.7])[5], as existence in this world wherein we are surrounded with imperfect and finite goods which cannot totally satisfy us:

> These things cannot be called flawless goods, since they do not endure permanently, are mixed with what is bad, and are not capable of satisfying desire completely . . . (1964, 8.3).

Conversely, the high good must be that which is permanent, unmixed with the bad, and capable of satisfying desire completely (1964).

In this life, humans are generally unable to distinguish the good from the bad because of sin—just as a diseased eye cannot make the distinction between light and dark that is easily discernible to the healthy eye (1964, 5.1). People live as if blind in the midst of imperfect goods, thinking them the true good. The goals humans set accordingly are finite, cannot be satisfying, and lead to lives of distraction and travel on the wrong path downward toward hell [1964, 11.15].

De Nobili poses the problem of the human condition in another way by saying that humans are inflicted with a disease named "desire":

> What is the cause for the human sickness? It is desire, desire for the pleasures of the body, for worldly honors, and for power[6] . . . Pleasure and pride and wealth[7] are the causes for the disease which is sin, and human desire is the obstacle to "reaching the shore"[8] and to loving (*bhakti*) the Lord of all. It is therefore necessary that humans renounce desire completely in order that there be no cause for sin; or at least that they moderate it so as to not leave the path of what is right [1964, 8.6].

The Incarnation as God's Response to the Human Condition

If humans thus find themselves ill with this disease of desire and spiritual blindness, God is the divine physician seeking a cure:

> The example of a divine physician who carefully reflects on what he should do, knowing that he must cure a great disease, is analogous to how the creator comprehended the right way to act in order to save humans, leading them to the shore of freedom. . . . The creator who by his very essence is mercy, takes as his form a human soul and body and comes into this world as a divine physician, as befits this boundless mercy [1964, 8.5].

This physician can offer two basic remedies for the plight from which humans suffer: *saṁnyāsa*, the complete renunciation of desire, as occurs in the fourth stage of life (*āśrama*), or the more minimal commitment to live with desire bound, limited by *dharma* [1964, 8.7]. By either path humans will find a way out of the dark world of desire.

But this "higher viewpoint" is simply unknown to humans who cannot see beyond the visible, so God in divine goodness decides to come down to present visibly the two things which must be seen, that "other shore of liberation" where lies the true happiness humans do not experience in this world, and the right path which we must travel in order to get there. The only way to present these unseen truths convincingly is for the divine physician to become the divine teacher on earth:

> The creator thus decided, "It is necessary to show this path," and so took on a human nature and walked the earth for a short time doing deeds of *dharma* as one with a holy vow (*vrata*) to do without the pleasures of women, etc., as one totally poor, as one rejecting worldly pride . . . . The creator, with a human nature, *walked the earth as the divine teacher, teaching all the works of* dharma, without forcing it upon the human mind and will which are by nature free, *making the full teaching of* dharma *by his flawless deeds and divine sermons, adjusting the difficulty to each (audience) so that each can reach the shore* [1964, 11.16] (Emphasis added).

The image of the teacher that emerges here must be set against the background of the previous discussion of imperfect goods, sin, and spiritual blindness and desire. To be a teacher involves a whole way of life, not merely words; the teacher seeks the soul, not merely the mind. Below I will discuss the specific context which must have come to the mind of listeners when de Nobili spoke in this fashion. First, however, let us see how he uses this idea of the teacher in contrast to the idea of *avatāra*.

The Conditions Imposed on the Incarnation and the Problem of Avatāras

The obvious corollary of what de Nobili has said thus far is that if the Incarnation is for the purpose of teaching humans a lesson, the teacher must be credible:

> If the divine physician came to implement these two means which remedy sin, he had to abandon pleasures in the body and soul which he took as his form, and experience suffering from meritorious asceticism, etc.; in teaching that wealth, etc. are undesirable he had to demonstrate complete poverty. To show that he loathed the pride of this world he has to

walk the earth as a poor man among the poor, without the pride of contact with kings, etc. . . . .

If the creator had ruled many kingdoms with his human body and soul, and experience [*sic*] pleasures like that of sex—how could he have taught the people, "Abandon desire for pleasure and wealth and worldly honors?" Or if he did teach it, if the people had seen in him actions contrary to his words, there would have been no good reason why they should have listened to his teaching, "Renounce desire for all these things" [1964, 8.8].

Thus the life of Jesus is understood as conformed to his teaching, not the other way around. People looking at his actions see the embodiment of what he was telling them to do: they could thus imitate this teacher and be like him: go with him to the other shore, liberation.

In this way de Nobili presents Jesus as the divine guru and thus identifies him with the most important local image of God, as we shall see below. On the immediate level two purposes are evident. First, it could explain why Jesus was not a king, not wealthy, and why he died a miserable death: this was to be expected, since he was a renunciant.

This also gives de Nobili his basis for criticizing the *avatāras* popular among the people: such appearances of God on earth would have to be marvelous events and therefore should have some marvelous purpose. But what can humans learn from a god who becomes a boar or a tortoise (as did Visnu), or from a god who takes human form and acts scandalously and without any of the attributes one would rightly expect of a god (as did Siva)? There is no evident salvific reason for such *avatāras*, and hence it makes no sense to assume that a god would undertake them.[9]

The Missionary as Guru

The theory and practice of missionary inculturation proposed by de Nobili is likewise given a firmer spiritual foundation when God is portrayed as a teacher and the incarnation as a teaching process. For de Nobili, the missionary is above all a guru, as this passage from near the end of the *Dūṣaṇa Tikkāram* illustrates:

Just as the highest action among the divine actions was the work of giving that teaching which helps souls toward reaching the shore [of salvation], it is no mistake to say that [for us] this work is precious compared to all others. That is to say, this is the most important work of the true teacher— apart from meditation and prayer and other such duties—and he must be greatly concerned that his work be fruitful, even if he should have no other work [1964, 30.1].

If God came down on earth to teach the way to salvation, the missionary as "another Christ" must likewise make visible in word and deed the same path to salvation. When explaining why missionaries must learn local languages, de Nobili makes clear the connection between God's work and the missionary's work:

> When the divine guru, our creator, left this world and, returned to heaven (*mokṣa*), he taught his disciples (*śisya*) to go forth into the world to make known to all the good news of his Veda. Because they could not perform the work given to them without learning the languages of the various peoples, he had [once only] given to the great-souled true teachers (*satguru*) the knowledge to teach the Veda in the languages of the various peoples. Those who were similarly good teachers went forth to make the Scripture [Veda] known, but did not dare to do this work without learning the languages of all those places. Likewise today the teachers must reflect carefully and fulfil their duty in this regard [1964, 32.21].

This reasoning can of course be extended to all aspects of adaptation: Christ adapted himself to the customs of dress, food, social structures, and the like of his time, in order to reach the people "where they were"; so too missionaries as teachers must suit the presentation of their message to their listeners.[10] We also glimpse here the spiritual outlook which gave de Nobili himself the strength to do his work for so many years: in becoming an ascetic and renunciant in the Hindu manner, he was simply a disciple of his teacher, Christ himself; he was simply imitating the Incarnation.

Contextualization and the Significance of de Nobili's Exposition of Christ as Guru

I have thus examined a primary way in which de Nobili presents the Christian mystery and must now assess [1] its significance against the background of the thought de Nobili "brought with him" to India; [2] its likely significance in the context of contemporary Hindu thought; and [3] the way in which the contextualization gave his Christian position a new understanding.

The European Background of de Nobili's Position

I do not mean to suggest that de Nobili borrowed certain discrete, definite "ideas" from Indian religions that he could have found nowhere else and were totally foreign to the European tradition.[11] Indeed, there are many biblical and European precedents regarding the teacher which might be understood as background for de Nobili's presentation of Christ as guru or teacher, of which I wish to give only a single apt example here.

It is not surprising that de Nobili, as a Jesuit, stresses the exemplary role of the life of Christ, since this was greatly stressed in the writings of his "master,"

Ignatius of Loyola.[12] In the *Constitutions* of the Jesuit Order, for instance, Ignatius explains the exemplary role of the life of Christ in general and in particular for those who would be Jesuits:

> It is likewise highly important to bring this to the mind of those who are being examined . . . to how great a degree it helps and profits one in the spiritual life to abhor in its totality and not in part whatever the world loves and embraces, and to accept and desire with all possible energy whatever Christ our Lord has loved and embraced . . . [Followers of Christ] desire to clothe themselves with the same clothing and uniform of their Lord because of the love and reverence which He deserves, to such an extent that where there would be no offense to His Divine Majesty and no imputation of sin to the neighbor, they would wish to suffer injuries, false accusations, and affronts, and to be held and esteemed fools . . . because of their desire to resemble and imitate in some manner our Creator and Lord Jesus Christ, by putting on His clothing and uniform, since it was for our spiritual profit that He clothed Himself as He did. For He gave us an example that in all things possible to us we might seek, through the aid of His grace, to imitate and follow Him, since He is the way which leads men to life [*Constitution*, 1970: 4.44].

Just as in the *Dūṣaṇa Tikkāram*, de Nobili describes the Incarnation as the way in which God came to teach humans that they must end desire for pleasure, power, and honors, Christ teaches a way opposite to that of the "world," a way the Incarnation and Christ's example have made it possible for us to follow.

But the European tradition has always been uncomfortable with attributing too much soteriological significance to the idea of Christ as teacher, since this might imply that sin is merely ignorance and that the real goal of the Incarnation is the imparting of knowledge. The "shadow" of Platonism was always there to be avoided, and the sacrificial theory of the death of Christ is usually given precedence over the exemplary role of his life. De Nobili to some extent avoids the danger by emphasizing that it is desire, not ignorance, which is the source of sin. He does not hesitate to speak of sin in fairly traditional terms. But the more important point for our purposes is that there is an Indian model for de Nobili's portrayal of the Incarnation which itself intends to avoid the reduction of salvation to the mere imparting of knowledge: the idea of the guru.[13]

A Possible Hindu Context: Śaiva Siddhānta and God as Guru

It is risky enough to offer an interpretation of the position of someone such as de Nobili based simply on a reading of one work, and conclusions drawn must remain tentative and open to revision. It is all the more risky then to move toward comparative study in an effort to identify aspects of de Nobili's thought which derive from the Indian context. What is said here regarding the similarities and differences between de Nobili's position and that of the Śaiva Siddhānta must be especially marked with an openness to revision.

In the time of de Nobili, South Indian Hinduism flourished in three basic forms: Vaiṣṇavism, oriented to the worship of Visnu and forms of Visnu like Kṛṣṇa; goddess worship oriented to the worship of great goddesses such as Mīnākṣī in the great Madurai temple, or to the almost infinite variety of local village goddesses; and Śaivism, oriented to the worship of Śiva.

De Nobili ignored goddess worship, probably writing it off as mere idolatry. He seems to have had some contact with the Vaiṣṇavas, but more with the Śaivites, in particular with Śaivism's most prominent theological form in the Tamil area, the Śaiva Siddhānta. When de Nobili quotes from Hindu texts or refers to Hindu myths, it is most often, I believe, from Saivite sources rather than Vaiṣṇava ones.[14]

One of the most significant points in the Śaiva Śiddhānta is the school's development of the idea that Śiva, the immaterial and utterly transcendent God, saves the human race as a guru or teacher. While the Śaiva Śiddhāntins by no means invented the guru idea, their explanation of Śiva as guru brings the notion to a culmination of theological elaboration (Pope, xliv).

This is not the place for an extended elaboration of the Śaiva Śiddhānta, even regarding the guru idea. I will rely on a useful analysis by G.U. Pope of a section of an important Śaivite work, the *Tiruvaruṭpayan* (ca. 1307 c.e.) of *Umapati,* to demonstrate how the Siddhāntins used the idea of divine guru. The relevant section of the text (verses 41–49) may be summarized as follows, according to its commentaries.[15]

5.41. In order to make invisible, indwelling grace visible, God assumes the bodily form of a guru.[16]

5.42. Only the indwelling Śiva can discern the disease of the human condition; he comes as guru to heal it.[17]

5.43. He is concealed in the guise of guru, and appears as a human, unrecognizable to all unless he further reveals his identity.

5.44. Humans cannot recognize the guru or his grace, because they are immersed in the darkness of sense perception.

5.45. Just as hunters use lures in the form of the animal to be caught lest the animal be frightened away, so too God comes in the guru form to "snare" humans who would be terrified to see his full divinity.[18]

5.48. To those who are freed already from deception, he is revealed in their inner consciousness; to those immersed in the sense world, he must come as the visible guru.

5.49. No one can know the way of freedom unless the guru reveals it.

5.50. No matter how ready or how wise one may be, (salvific) knowledge will not come to a person without the grace of the guru; even a perfect crystal will not gleam without the sunlight refracted in it.

While this text does not explain exactly how the divine guru is revealed in human form—the human guru(s) seem(s) both to be and not to be Śiva at the same time, both a revelation of Śiva and a concealment—other texts do state that Śiva graciously reveals himself to beings in various ways, depending on their knowledge. The guru form is for those incapable of more direct revelation of the divine. M. Dhavamony explains the teaching procedure according to Meykanta Tevar's *Śivañānapotam* (1221 c.e.):

> God whose love for souls is at first hidden in them like the shadow of water in water, condescends ultimately to reveal his love in a visible form; no one would know it if he did not reveal it . . . The divine manifestation in the form of a guru takes place in many ways. To *vinnanakalar* he appears himself as true wisdom, and illumines their minds from within. He appears before the *piralayakalar* as a guru in Śaiva-form, four-armed, three-eyed, black-throated, and performing the three functions;[19] and he imparts knowledge. To the ignorant *cakalar* he revealed *nanam*, concealing himself as a guru whose form is similar to theirs [Dhavamony, 215].[20]

The divine teacher reveals himself according to the capacity of those he wishes to save, taking on an embodied form for the sake of human beings (*cakalar*).[21] The references to teaching and ignorance may naturally make one think of a kind of gnosticism, but it is clear that the Śaiva Siddhānta is talking about a mysterious and gracious salvific process involving the definite intervention of God from outside. This "teacher" does not save through mere wise ideas.

It is necessary for many reasons to reject the temptation to equate this view with de Nobili's view of the Incarnation. Most immediately, it is a fact that the general theological and anthropological terms in which the Śaivite and Christian traditions express their soteriologies are different enough to caution us against any kind of facile equivalence. Nevertheless it is possible that de Nobili turned to this local Śaiva Siddhānta theology when looking for terms in which to explain what the Incarnation was all about. Portraying Christ as a guru helped make the gospel intelligible. It might be added, too, that the complex relationship between the divine and the human guru(s) in the Siddhānta could serve as an analogy for the relationship between Christ the divine guru and the gurus who are missionaries in India.

A final reference to the Siddhānta tradition is that when de Nobili criticizes the *avatāra* theory and says that the Incarnation is not at all like an *avatāra*, he is (consciously or not) adopting the position of the Siddhāntins who reject the *avatāra* theory in favor of that of Śiva as guru. Bror Tiliander, in his *Christian and Hindu Terminology*, points out that when many early missionaries were reluctant to equate the incarnation with *avatāra*, this view was not foreign to Indian thought: "the Śaiva theism, e.g., is not dependent on Śiva in the form of an *avatāra*." Describing God's earthly presence by the theory of *avatāra* did not appeal to Śaivites (105), and indeed, "there is no room for the *Avatāra*-concept in Śaiva-theism" (106). He explains:

> This may be due to the transcendent trend. Śiva stands outside his creation of which he is only a *causa efficiens*. Incarnation would make

him subject to Karma and Saṁsāra, over which he is ruler. But in order to help his devotees to reach the final goal, the complete union with Śiva, he occasionally assumes a human shape and appears in disguise, as a religious preceptor, as a Guru, often with the name Satguru, "the true Guru." Schomerus points out that Śiva as Guru is identical with that Śiva who is present in the soul and connected with the soul in a very close union (107).

De Nobili is thus, in effect, taking sides in a Hindu theological debate, standing with the Śaivites over against the Vaiṣṇavas.[22] His choice of the image of guru in his act of contextualization carried with it the "threads" of the whole fabric from which it was "excised." In the next section I must raise the question of whether or not this contextualization was fruitful and theologically defensible.

Assessing de Nobili's Theology against Its Hindu Background: De Nobili as Theological Innovator

On the practical level de Nobili's adoption of the guru image was probably as useful and successful as his decision to observe caste restrictions regarding food, and so forth, to present himself as a renunciant according to the ideals of Hindu society, and to allow converts to retain many details of their pre-Christian lives. By describing himself as a guru sent forth by the divine guru to spread the Veda, de Nobili enabled Hindus to situate him and his God with respect to their own culture and religion. This new god and new visitor were not invading kings, but could be counted among those mysterious teachers who sometimes appear on this earth. Even if de Nobili would reinterpret the term "guru," just as he did Hindu social customs, his use of the term was a legitimate adaptation for the sake of opening communication. As suggested above, it must also have been personally attractive, for a self-understanding as guru in imitation of the divine would enable de Nobili to explain his delicate balancing act: his immersion in the culture and his duty to say something to the culture.

His approach to the Śaivite context provided de Nobili with an incarnational theology which was both salvific and demythologized; a way to present Christ intelligibly for a Hindu audience, yet as unique. Just as there is ultimately only one guru for the Śaivite, there is only one Christ for the Christian, whereas, in contrast to both, the *avatāras* of Visnu are, in theory, endlessly repeatable manifestations.

Likewise, the problem of direct iconic presentation of the divine is averted, since the guru is not meant to resemble God in any material way: the teaching is revealed through hiddenness. In Christ the divine guru shows us the way to salvation, while yet remaining within the constraints of the hiddenness of his life and death.

We have seen too that from a Hindu viewpoint salvation through a guru is not equivalent to being saved by knowledge imparted by a "teacher." Salvation is not a question of what one knows, but of a new perspective on a newly illumined world. The presence of the guru (Śiva or the human guru who somehow presents Śiva) is itself an event of divine grace, and his communication with his student or disciple (śisya) is revelation, the presenting of Śiva through the "concealment" of the person of the teacher, so that the human recipient is gradually enabled to receive the saving truth.

To summarize: the Śaivite idea of the guru is founded on the particular way in which Śiva, through the human relationship of guru and student and by any word or image or action which might be used within the confines of that relationship, gradually reveals the way to salvation in a concealment adjusted to human eyes. It is nonmythological and aniconic, since the human form of Śiva is not understood to replicate the divine in any direct fashion; in fact it would not be salvific if it did directly adequate the divine to what is intelligible to humans. It is intrinsic to the aniconic nature of the embodiment in the guru that we are not supposed to visualize it as a direct garbing of Śiva with a human form or forms, since that visualization too would be nonsalvific.

This background needs specification and filling out by further study, but it should be clear that calling Christ "guru" is not the same as calling him "teacher"; this new appellation is really the beginning of an effort to understand Christ within the context of a whole new set of concepts and spiritual possibilities. That is to say, by utilizing the concept of guru, de Nobili is not only making something new intelligible to the Hindu, but is also thinking and saying something new about Christ that had never been said before. Christ is the guru: the "concealing revelation" of God among humans through the medium of human relationships, the salvific yet demythologized and aniconic presence of the divine in the human.

De Nobili's contextualization thereby offers Christian theology (not just in India, but everywhere in the world!) the way toward a better utilization of the salvific/exemplary ideal that was never quite satisfactorily embodied in the tradition of Christ the teacher, the imitation of Christ, and so on. This contextualization would be a boon to the entire Christian community; it would help Christians to understand Christ better by affording us a new set of rational constructs—words, ideas, images, wider connections with other schools of thought—through which to study and think about the Christ event.[23]

Implications for the Theory and Practice of Contextualization Today

This chapter has presented a single specific example in detail. I have avoided more general comments on the theme of contextualization, because of my convictions that (1) every case of contextualization is an individual one, occurring in a certain time and place; each is interesting precisely because it is local, and (2) a general theory of contextualization must be generated only from a careful examination of local cases.

I should like to conclude with a few reflections on the implications of what I have said thus far. To begin with, de Nobili's example makes it quite clear that something like what we today call "contextualization" or "inculturation" has been going on for quite a long time—beginning with the Incarnation itself, as he might say![24] Our places of contextualization have changed, and are often found "at home" and not in far-off "mission fields"; we are part of a long tradition, and must learn from our predecessors (of whom de Nobili is only one example), and not see ourselves as doing something "totally new" or "modern."

The example of de Nobili should remind us that tasks of contextualization are neither lightly assumed nor easily finished. It took de Nobili more than forty years in Madurai to accomplish what he did, and neither he nor anyone else has yet completed even his limited assimilation of the theology of the Śaiva Siddhānta. Whether in the "field" or in the "study" the person who seeks to cross cultural boundaries should be prepared for the "long haul," and be skeptical regarding the likelihood or value of quick results.

It is conversely the case that one cannot casually assume competence to judge the contextualization that someone else has tried to effect. An initial opinion might be that de Nobili was merely introducing to India the concept of "Christ as teacher," with all the strengths and weaknesses that idea had in the European tradition. But further study suggests that one cannot competently evaluate his concept of "Christ as guru" without knowledge of the Śaiva Siddhānta and the traditions behind that sixteenth-century school of theology. Localized expertise is required to judge the real value of a local contextualization.[25] Knowledge of one's own tradition is simply not adequate to an evaluation of what is truly a new development in theology, introduced from outside traditional sources.[26]

If one then steps back and views the virtually unlimited set of possible contextualizations, and also realizes that everybody's theological position is a contextualization, it becomes evident that a theologian cannot attempt to work out an entire systematic theology independently, relying solely on the evidence of his or her own traditional contextualization of the faith. Attention to the global plurality of contextualizations of the faith is neither a peripheral nor a subordinate discipline of theology; it has to do with the very core and substance of our understanding of our faith, in regard to which the intellectual framework of the European tradition is not essentially normative. There seems, then, to be little justification for assuming today that one can simply consult traditional and European theological resources to express what our faith is all about.

I mean this fairly specifically too: for instance, even a Christologist who lives in Boston and has no interest in going to India at all is not a very good theologian if he or she does not take an interest in a claim such as "Christ is the guru." There is no good theological reason for not being interested! Even if each of us is limited in time and resources and must choose what we are going to focus on, we must nevertheless be more conscious in our choices and more explicit in our justifications for the contexts we attend to or do not attend to.

If we admit furthermore that if it is a rare scholar who has mastered even one denomination's theology, much less that of the other Christian churches, we can also see that no one can master completely what has happened in Africa, India, Japan, and elsewhere, when Christians like de Nobili rethought the Christian message in a non-Christian context. Theologians and specialists in various cultures and religions will have to depend on one another, and theology will have to become a fundamentally collaborative effort. It will become commonplace to ask a theologian what "research team" he or she is part of— as is already commonplace in the sciences.[27]

The challenge to the way we normally do theology is thus enormous, but de Nobili's example should encourage us by showing us the positive side of the challenge. His insight into Christ as guru is an enormously rich one which could help (I say "could," for it is not inevitable that this will happen in the near future) the Christian community throughout the world to learn to see Christ in a new way, more completely than has hitherto been possible in our history. It could help theologians in the construction of new technical vocabularies for Christology and in gaining a new objectivity regarding certain traditional theological notions such as "Christ the teacher." De Nobili has in effect made the riches of the Śaiva Siddhānta part of the theological heritage of the church.

Most generally, the message of de Nobili is that when God crossed the vast boundary between the divine and the human, we were taught to do the same, crossing the small boundaries among our many cultures and religions. If we can believe the still truly surprising news that European culture has illuminated our experience of Christ, surely we need not be surprised that the cultures of every part of the world are waiting, now impatiently, to offer their own illuminations.

Notes

1. This raises the question of what exactly de Nobili understood himself to be doing, in an age before ideas like the "variety of cultures" were commonplace, and whether or not he can be thought to have done what we think we are doing today, if he did not have the words and concepts we use. Because answering these questions would lead me far beyond the confines of this paper, I will simply have to proceed with the "caution about differences" in mind. In an earlier (unpublished) paper I have attempted to explore in some detail the encounter of de Nobili's Renaissance-Reformation worldview with that of seventeenth-century Tamil Hinduism.

2. Throughout, I will refer generally to "inculturation" and "contextualization" interchangeably, and mean the effort by a person of one culture to represent something discovered in the "home" culture in the appearances, images, words, customs of the other culture. As the title of this essay suggests, I do not claim to deal with the entirety of de Nobili's works (which are not translated from the Tamil). The *Dūṣaṇa Tikkāram* "Refutation of calumnies") comes somewhat late in his career, and was perhaps written while he was in prison during 1640. Rajamanickam indicates that there was a Sanskrit text (not extant) before the Tamil text available to us.

(See Rajamanickam, 1972:124.) Any translations from the Tamil are my own, and section references are to Rajamanickam's editions of the *Dūṣaṇa Tikkāram* and de Nobili's other works.

3. These points are explained with great sophistication in certain (Vaiṣṇava) schools of thought. Since de Nobili does not refer in *Dūṣaṇa Tikkāram* to any of the specific theological defenses of *avatāra*, references in this chapter should be understood to refer only to the more popular notion of God's putting various material forms for salvific purposes.

4. Later chapters defend the idea of a virgin birth (chapter 9), Jesus' life of poverty (chapter 10), and the need for his passion and death (chapter 11). Chapter 12 concludes the argument by comparing his life with that of the mythological *avatāras* of the gods.

5. References are made here to the chapter sections enumerated in Rajamanickam's edition.

6. These three desires must remind us of the trio already familiar in de Nobili's Jesuit tradition: the temptations to riches, honors and pride described in Ignatius' "Meditation on the Two Standards" in his *Spiritual Exercises*. This single example should again remind us that any attention I give to Hindu sources for de Nobili's thought is not meant to preclude European roots as well; indeed, it is probable, in learning from sources outside one's own culture, that, at least when first exploring a new idea, one will approximate something from one's own tradition.

7. Notice that the third desire is first given as the desire for power (*aiśvarya*) and then for wealth (*danam*).

8. *Karai ēru*, or *mokṣakarai ēru*, is the way de Nobili describes salvation in the *Dūṣaṇa Tikkāram*. The image is either that of crossing a river to the opposite shore, or getting out of a lake to the shore; in either case, at least according to the Hindu image, the water is this world, *saṃsāra*.

9. See de Nobili's mocking reference to the animal *avatāras* in 6.2, and the argument against the *avatāras* in chapter 12. The entire idea is set forth succinctly in the *Kaṭavuḷ Nirṇayam*, where de Nobili gives a definition of God and shows how the deities described in the *avatāra* stories could not possibly measure up to the standard of that definition.

10. In his two Latin works addressed to authorities in Goa and Rome in defense of his methods, he appeals to the example of Christ who tolerated the social biases of his people; as for instance when he refrained almost entirely from a mission to the Gentiles, lest the Jewish people turn away from him. See, for instance, *Adaptation*, 23, 27, 83; and *Indian Customs*, 126, 153.

11. If that is ever possible. The idea of cross-cultural intelligibility presumes that those crossing over will recognize—correctly or not—elements resembling those of his own culture, and in any case it is fairly rare, I would suspect, that any person think an idea totally unknown to the thinking of other cultures.

12. Ignatius himself, of course, drew on the venerable theme of the "imitation of Christ."

13. Some significant differences cannot be explored here—e.g., Ignatius' text lacks the sharp and very Indian emphasis found in the *Dūṣaṇa Tikkāram* on the role of desire as the source of three sins. It is more important for my purpose and in keeping with what follows to note that although the Indian notion of the guru is conceptually at least quite the opposite of a "cult of personality," the imitation Ignatius suggests focuses ultimately on the idea of being with Christ—almost for its own sake; but in the

Dūṣaṇa Tikkāram what matters is what Jesus stands for, *the way* he points to by his example. The person of the teacher does not become the center of attention.

14. See for instance the *Kaṭavul Nirṇayam*, where it is Śaivite myths which de Nobili ridicules in terms of the images of the divine that one would glean from them; and the *Ñānopadeśa Kurippiḍam*, wherein de Nobili cites a large number of Tamil verses, probably of Śaivite origin. Cronin (60) suggests that Śaivism was the main religion of Madurai in de Nobili's time. But it is more correct to say that it predominated over its theological rival, Vaiṣṇavism. In practice, goddess-worship probably attracted the most devotees.

15. Pope elaborates the verses of *Umāpati* with the aid of a traditional commentary. The Tamil of *Umāpati*, the (same?) commentary, and a modern elucidation of both by Ramanathapillai are found in the Śaiva Siddhānta Society's 1968 edition of the *Tiruvaruṭpayan*.

16. The text described here does not explain exactly the relationship between the divine guru and the one or more human gurus. In brief, one might say that the human guru is not simply Śiva, but nevertheless has no relevance apart from Śiva. There may be many gurus, but all of them are really just the embodiment of the one guru, Śiva.

17. Recall how de Nobili made the same connection between healer and teacher.

18. It is interesting that de Nobili makes the same analogy in his *Ñānopadeśa Kurippiḍam*: "If you wonder who [God chose to save us through incarnation], it is like when someone catching birds catches them if he puts out [as a lure] a bird of the same kind [as the one he is attempting to catch], not a bird which is its enemy. Likewise, he decided to give *mokṣa* and show the way to *mokṣa* by taking on this human nature, because man had, in this human nature, turned against God"(12.3).

19. It is interesting that what might appear to us as the more material, mythical manifestation is preserved for those who are of higher knowledge: the mythical appearance is a higher "concealment," for the sake of those who do not need the clear, exact human form.

20. Conscious beings are divided into the three groups (*viññānakalar, piraḷayakalar* and *cakalar*) according to whether they have one or more of the three "defects"; *āṇava* (ignorance), *karma* (the fruits of past deeds), and *māyai* (immersion in the material). The viññānakalar are bound only by *āṇava*, the *piraḷayakalar* by *āṇava* and *karma*, and the *cakalar* by all three.

21. Compare with de Nobili's description in 11.16 of the *Dūṣaṇa Tikkāram*, cited above, on how Jesus adapted his teaching to his various audiences.

22. Even though, as pointed out, it is a Śaivite variation on the *avatāra* theme which de Nobili mocks in the *Kaṭavul Nirṇayam*. It is important to remember as well that the Vaiṣṇava theory is not a materialistic one (such that God has a body in the ordinary sense), but is a highly developed alternative to the Śaivite view. De Nobili was perhaps not familiar with true Vaiṣṇava theology.

23. One wants to claim that de Nobili's use of the term "guru" is more than a practical strategy, contextualized theology and theology done across cultural boundaries become constitutive parts of systematic theology—and therefore rightly subject to the same scrutiny any other theological idea is subject to, even apart from the original context. One will next have to assess the larger and pan-Indian notion of the guru—which is not identical with nor reducible to the Śaiva Siddhānta viewpoint—and ask whether saying "Christ is guru" is a universally appropriate, meaningful and accessible theological statement. So too, a more careful scrutiny of the Śaiva Siddhānta

will have to ask not only how that theology enriches our understanding of Christ once he is put in that context, but also what must be done about some theological problems that do arise—e.g., regarding the nature of the soul or the exact nature of the presence of Śiva in one or more human gurus, etc. This broader work remains to be done, but, it is my strong impression that de Nobili is sufficiently cautious that his synthesis could not be considered a kind of syncretism, nor as open to the charge of gnosticism or salvation-through-knowledge; and that he is even too cautious in exploring the possibilities of Śaiva Siddhānta not to mention the possibilities of Vaiṣṇavism and goddess-worship, which he left unexplored.

24. Even though the Europe of the 16th and 17th centuries had not yet formulated clear ideas of "cultures" and "religions," and de Nobili never used the terms we do for his project. It is arguable that therefore de Nobili was not "inculturating the gospel" because he had no word for this procedure, even if he was doing a great deal of what we have in mind today.

25. I say this without wishing to make the further and unwarranted claim that only the local expert has the right to judge the product of local theological reflection. What is articulated and rational and spiritual should, after all, be universally accessible in some fashion.

26. That is, if one takes inculturation tó mean anything more than an extrinsic adaptation of the nonessentials of the faith. If one has an a priori view that because of the absolute nature of Christian revelation nothing can be introduced to the faith from outside its tradition, the whole idea of inculturation is not really a theological issue at all.

27. This is true notwithstanding the example of de Nobili himself, who worked most of his life in isolation from other theologians. That kind of isolation is not likely to occur in today's world, and moreover, as a missionary de Nobili did not think of himself as doing something private. Trying to live in a new culture, he was in any case continually in dialogue with the Hindu theologians around him. This of course raises the question of whether or not one's theological community must consist of those with whom one shares faith.

References

Constitutions of the Society of Jesus. 1970. St. Louis: Institute of Jesuit Sources.

Cronin, A.J. 1959. *A Pearl to India.* London: Rupert Hart-Davis.

De Nobili, Roberto. 1964. *Dūṣaṇa Tikkāram* ("Refutation of calumnies"). Tuttukkuti. S. Rajamanickam, S.J. ed.

———. 1969. *Kaṭavuḷ Nirṇayam.* Palayamkottai, S. Rajamanickam, S.J., ed.

———. 1971. *Adaptation.* Palayamkottai: De Nobili Research Institute. S. Rajamanickam, S.J., ed.; J. Pujo, S.J., trans. from Latin.

———. 1972. *Indian Customs.* Palayamkottai: De Nobili Research Institute. S. Rajamanickam, S.J., ed.; J. Pujo, S.J., trans. from Latin.

Dhavamony, M. 1971. *Love of God according to Śaiva Siddhānta.* Oxford.

Pope, G.U. 1900. *The Trivuvācagam.* Oxford.

Rajamanickam, S. 1972. *The First Oriental Scholar.* Palayamkottai: De Nobili Research Institute.

Tiliander, Bror. 1974. *Christian and Hindu Terminology: A Study of Their Mutual Relations with Special Reference to the Tamil Area.* Uppsala: Almqvist and Wiksell.

CHAPTER 4

The Formation of a Missionary: Bartolomé de las Casas, 1484–1566

Francis Patrick Sullivan

The facts about the man can be set out swiftly. The interpretation, not so swiftly. He was born in Seville in 1484. His family got involved in Columbus' later voyages. He himself was abroad in 1502 on Haiti where he owned land and held natives. Ordained a priest back in Europe about 1509, he returned to the New World and the crisis of conscience raised by the Dominicans there starting in 1510—that is, the Conquest was immoral and unjust. He was converted to the Dominican vision in 1514. From then on he fashioned his own vision to defend the Amerindians against the Conquest. He did this first, by social planning, and then by entrance into the Dominican Order and by confrontation with *conquistador* ideas. He wrote "On the Only Way to Draw All Peoples to the Truth of Belief" in the late 1520s, a work he later expanded. It became the source of the Roman document *Sublimis Deus*, the charter for Roman Catholic missions. He was behind the creation of the New Laws in 1542, laws which were not fully kept until much later. He wrote "The Destruction of the Indies," as part of his effort toward the New Laws. He was bishop of Chiapas in 1544 when he wrote his "Rules for Confessors." He returned to the court in Spain in 1547 to spend the rest of his life there fighting the Amerindian cause. He defended the true humanness of the natives, again, against Juan Ginès de Supúlveda, in the early 1550s. His final efforts were still toward restoring integrity—spiritual, moral, political, economic—to the natives of the New World. From this period came his "On the Power of the King," and "On the Treasure of Peru." He made his case eventually to his own time, and makes it now to ours. But these facts need to be seen as a process or their full sense will not be clear.

Bartolomé de las Casas saw the New World for a long time without seeing it. He had been formed in Christianity, but it was a formation in institutional blindness, as it was for most of his Spanish contemporaries who came to colonize the Indies. Personally, he loved the Amerindians and treated them kindly. Yet Christianity is more than personal, it is institutional. The New World natives looked to most Europeans like barbarians no matter how sophisticated native cultures were. Therefore natives were all to be treated as barbarians. Superior beings could dispose of inferior beings as they wished. Las Casas was one of the superior beings. Something had to uncover the reality of native humanness to the reality of Christian seeing. What did it for Las Casas was Amerindian suffering and Christian compassion on an institutional scale.

The trigger for his conversion was what Christianity has always hoped it would be, a voice revealing how God felt about an actual situation. That voice had to be someone with a soul large enough to feel what God felt. The lineage of such voices goes back to Christ, back beyond Christ to Hebrew prophets and to Greek thinkers who knew there had to be a justice to existence or existence was pure and simple madness. The voice which came to Las Casas was that of the Dominicans in Haiti. He saw the mortal sin of the exploitation of the natives after observing its results for a year and a half (1510). Yet there was something of charity already at work in him, a behavior toward New World natives that was respectful of them, though within a situation which he would later call mortal sin.

Pedro de Córdoba was the conscious ideal of Las Casas. He was pure Christianity in practice for the salvation of others. Las Casas' description of him uses the classic terms for that sanctity, early vocation, great gifts, self-surrender to mortification, prayer, rigorous rule of life, then exteriorization of that intense inner life through an ecclesial form into the corporal and spiritual works of mercy. Such sanctity awes those who see it. Las Casas draws a vivid picture of Córdoba as the very first to preach to the Amerindians in Haiti—and this, many years after the Spaniards had conquered the island. Córdoba is seated. He preaches through an interpreter. He narrates the history of the world up to its culminating moment, the death of Jesus on the cross. Then Córdoba goes away, leaving an example of what should be done.

But Las Casas does not really do this. He creates agricultural schemes first of all, to try to change the master/slave relationship (1519). When that seems to fail, he gathers knowledge about Amerindian life that will change the conqueror's attitude (1524–1539). When that seems to fail, he resorts to laws to prevent slavery. When that seems to fail, he tries to change all laws about the Indies into new ones (1542). When eventually that seems to fail, he creates a confessional doctrine to work on the conscience of the conqueror mightily (1547). When that seems to fail, he argues to a standstill all view of Amerindians that justify Spanish barbarity against them (1550). When that seems to fail, he argues to the right of all oppressed peoples to be free of their oppressing lords, spiritual or temporal (1558). In the process he meets the Amerindian face to face on many an occasion. He learns that truth and goodness are the only means either Amerindian or Spaniard has in order to meet and to live with each other. He learns the tragedy of mistakes, his own particularly, not just about black African slavery, the mistake he was bitterly sorry for later, but about trusting spiritual goals to worldly people, trusting political goals to kings who were heavily in debt, trusting the delicate beauty of Jesus Christ to church officials who thought like conquerors. The seeming failures were partial successes, though he could not achieve his ultimate goal, the total freedom of the Amerindians.

A passion for beauty is what Las Casas has. The horror he comes to see makes him conscious of his heritage and of his senses. He uses both to restore the beauty given by God to every human being, Spaniard and Amerindian alike. To the Spaniard he preaches justice; to the Amerindian, the truth and goodness of God—and to both, the harmony of eternal life. But not in these abstract terms; in concrete ones. There has never been a justifying reason for Spaniards to war against anyone in the New World. Therefore there is no justifying reason for Spain to rule or to profit from the New World in any way. Therefore its presence is grave sin whose outcome is damnation unless Spain restores all that it took or makes up for what it took in some other way. Lives cannot be restored, but the living can accept in their stead. Amerindian nations lack a sense of Christian charity, the charity that humanizes every element of personal and social life. They lack a sense of community with other nations. They lack a sense of justice based on that community, and a sense of charity that goes beyond their national confines. The two, Spaniard and Amerindian, must come to an absolute respect for each other. If not, the beauty of human being in its nature and its calling to eternal life will be marred to the point where the human being becomes a source of damnation instead, for victim as well as victimizer.

The vision is staggering in the circumstances of Las Casas' life. Both Spaniards and Amerindians were grooved into horrible life patterns by the time Las Casas woke up. The patterns of horror intensified and spread in each year of his life. He had to use the vision as best he could from crisis to crisis: the stubborn continuance of the *encomienda* system, despite modification, the continuance of the forbidden slave system, the resurgent use of wars of conquest, the continual treatment of Amerindians as forced labor under a different name, the fixed judgment on them as perpetual children or as out-and-out subhumans.

The vision becomes the source of social planning—for Amerindians to live near Spaniards and to profit from them as the Spaniards would profit from the Amerindians. The vision is his source for antislavery legislation. It is the source of his great missionary document, "On the Only Way to Draw All Peoples to the Truth of Belief." It is the source of law. It suffuses the New Laws he caused to be written and promulgated. It is the source of his doctrine on confession. It is the source of his great argument against Supúlveda about whether Amerindians are natural subjects for the superior Spanish beings. It is the source of his belief in total political freedom for conquered peoples. It is the source of all his moral doctrine. Human nature is made for goodness and truth; it is made for salvation and life with God. Goodness and truth are here on earth where salvation is worked out or lost. The life of God is found in the way we treat each other, or the way we restore each other if we can. He did argue for total restitution, total satisfaction for wrongs committed, fully believing that such action could restore the Spanish/Amerindian relationship to what it ought to be, a sharing of the Christian vision of salvation—something worked out here as the model for the hereafter.

His senses were opened as much as was his mind. Las Casas' language is often near the breaking point when he describes the horrors inflicted on Amerindians. And often also when he describes Amerindians bodily, spiritually, and their lands and some of their customs. What he has learned from the testimony of others he re-creates in his imagination of compassion so that he expresses himself as though he were an eyewitness. Those who read him only in later times think he is hysterical. Those who read stacks of testimony from that period know he is not. The purpose he had in expressing so vividly what had happened was to create an experience in the minds of those who had power over what was happening far away from their seats of power. Las Casas sensed that since both those who suffered and those who caused the suffering were human beings, if the cause (the oppressors) could ever know the effect (the oppression they caused), they would shift to compassion or they would know how they courted damnation. The accomplice also could not escape the choice, and the whole of Spain was an accomplice in mortal sin.

The language of the senses that Las Casas uses is a language meant to describe the full human being. Only after speaking of Spaniard and Amerindian as fully human does he use a language fitted to beasts and bestial behavior or brute suffering. The purpose he has in mind is complex and sophisticated: mutual recognition between Spaniard and Amerindian—even to the point where he hopes the Amerindian who sees the Spaniard making total restitution and satisfaction will see deeper and know it is the power of Christ that can change even brute conquerors into brethren. That might salvage the original purpose for which a pope gave Spain the privilege of entering the New World in the name of the church, and even to the further point where he hopes the Spaniard will see how precious the very differences between peoples are and will learn to live with differences as an equal, not as a superior.

Las Casas' hope is even deeper, though it seems to contradict the hope just described; he hopes that if cohabitation is impossible, Spain will leave, Christianity will leave, and God will use means other than Spanish Christianity to bring about Amerindian salvation. That would be the ultimate act of truth and goodness.

The ultimate expression of Las Casas' requirements for a missioner is that the missioner wants no power over people, no money from them, that the missioner love them with the charity practiced by Christ, and finally that the life of the missioner be in holiness what the message is in words.

All of this comes from Las Casas' sensing how Spanish Christianity has landed on the bodies and souls of the natives of the New World—and sensing it through the graphic testimony of so many who supplied him with descriptions of what was going on.

The passion of God is like a contradiction. Las Casas recognized his complicity, unwitting as it was, in the deaths of people, his acquiescence in a plan to release Haitian natives by introducing African slaves. Years later, he senses how his own soul is tied to the souls of others and he fears the loss of it along with those of other cooperators. It is as if there is a common soul to evil, as much as there is to goodness, even if the self is conscious of being individual. Las Casas tells confessors not to absolve dying conquistadors unless they free the people they own, give back all goods gotten from or through these people and restore the goods of others that they have destroyed.

Being tied personally to communal life and death is the essence of Las Casas' defense of the Amerindians, and his defense of the true nature of Christianity. It is this experience which makes the traditions of Christianity and rationality available to him. He can recognize that the integrity of every group and every individual is based on a community of nature and a community of redemption. He can see that differences in groups and persons are expressions of nature and expressions of redemption. He can see the Amerindians for what they are, and what they wish to be. He can interpret them and see what he and Christianity could possibly offer them. He can also see Christianity for what it is, and what it wishes to be. If all he can do is bring a violent, self-contradictory Christianity to a violent, self-contradictory Indian culture, he will do nothing. He will not associate violence with God. He will leave it to God to save that other culture by its own elements. He wants to bring life, and that only. Or he wants to receive life from those others, and that only. All his political and ecclesiastical work over a span of fifty years, early mistakes included, are based upon that desire.

Human nature is beautiful to Las Casas. In abstract terms this nature is mind, will, imagination, emotion, sensation, memory, sociability. In biblical terms this nature is called image of God, wanderer, chosen, redeemed, adopted, transfigured, lost. These are universal images: they can be offered to all people. Philosophical and biblical terms are born of experience and it is experience which brings them into play—not as ways to remember what one knew before experience, but as ways to practice a living relationship toward another, whether individual or group. Intelligence recognizes intelligence, freedom recognizes freedom, though these may not be someone else's terms, and though someone else may be an enemy. Philosophical and biblical terms are ways into a relationship, a relationship that then creates its own history as did the church of Rome with the culture it inherited from pagandom.

He could surely see the inhumanity of Amerindian behavior as well as that of Spanish. To him the practice of human sacrifice was an absolute sin, as absolute a sin as the unjust wars the Spaniards waged, as the *encomienda* system they imposed, as the genocide they practiced wittingly or unwittingly. He sought to understand, to get at the root reason why Amerindian and

Spaniard did what they did—the Amerindian, he said, for religious reasons, horrible as those reasons may be, and the Spaniard for a mixture of religious and worldly reasons as exemplified in the motivations of Cortés or the attitudes of Supúlveda. Las Casas also knew the larger defects of civilizations that lacked a sense of justice, the kind that comes, he thought, only with the revelation of Jesus Christ, the justice called the kingdom of God. And few European nations, if any, measured up to the justice of the kingdom of God brought by Christ.

The vision of Las Casas can now be seen as primordial, not archetypal and outside history. It is closer to the life of human beings than are the political and religious structures which pretend to bring ultimate meaning to life. For Las Casas, ultimate meaning was the physical and moral and imaginative and emotional integrity of individuals and of groups of people. And that integrity meant openness, even to the greatest differences. Because integrity is a function of truth and goodness: The right to know; the right to choose. This personal/social integrity is given in creation. It is never lost in falls from grace. This integrity is what grace comes to when grace returns seeking its own kind. This integrity forms the kingdom, here below first, in the heavens afterward. It has always been a gift, never a coercion.

Christianity and Spanish culture were privileged means for Las Casas. They were bearers of Christ. But Christ was as delicate a beauty as was the humanity Christ became one with. So if Christianity and Spanish culture bore another kind of Christ, even in the least bit against created nature or the mercy of salvation, then the bearers lost their privilege. They had to be evangelized to bring them back to the delicate beauty they had deformed. This judgment of Las Casas could well breed despair in Spanish Christian missioners who knew what everyone knows, that the best of people are beset with ignorance and other limitations, moral and physical, etc. It is to those unaware of self-evident truths that Las Casas directs his judgment. Humans absorb mistakes; they do not absorb contradictions. Christianity and Spanish culture remain privileged means for Las Casas until the moment they become a permanent threat to grace in Jesus Christ. Amerindian cultures are also privileged means for him until the moment they become a permanent threat to the integrity of their peoples. Aztec human sacrifice was such a threat. Closed societies were such a threat. Each society had to be a window on all societies.

There was a law of nations as well as a natural law, however tenuous both were and difficult to construe. That is why Las Casas saw a reverse influence possible from Amerindian cultures on Christianity. Amerindians could bring Spaniards to a consciousness of the meaning of their own Christianity and bring them to a consciousness of the presence of grace outside Spanish/Christian forms, and to a consciousness of the presence of created nature apart from their own. The Amerindians could even bring them to see the positive values of different religious experiences. Las Casas wrote of the differences, but not so that the Spanish Christian mind could know what to root out from the pagan soul in order to create the clean slate necessary for the name

"Christian" to be written on it without fear of contamination. He wrote to reveal the pagan soul, so that Spaniards would not think of it as subhuman and godless, and behave toward it in a subhuman, godless way.

Las Casas becomes an ideal missioner for his own time. It is in the meeting with the other that he overcomes the temptation to power. He turns to social service. He overcomes the temptation to greed by seeing how greed strips flesh and blood from victim and victimizer. He turns to social welfare. He overcomes the temptation to scorn the other as barbaric because of the effects of defamation and the demonic rights that defamers assume over the defamed. He turns to representing the truth about the other and about the conqueror. He writes history. He overcomes the temptation to lovelessness by loving what he sees and suffering the consequences of seeing what he loves destroyed by lovelessness. He turns to the charity revealed by Jesus Christ, the charity that sees all flesh and blood as one, that heals it, comforts its, defends it, frees it, confronts it, not as God would, but as a brother or sister would who had the same love as the parents. He overcomes the temptation to the holy life for the sake of God and his own soul. He turns to the holy life that is led for the sake of the brethren, seeking holiness as a consequence of the works of mercy—not in terms of seeking gain and loss of grace for the self, but in the likeness of the parables told by Jesus, the good Samaritan, the good shepherd, the lord of the vineyard, the prodigal, though more the father than the son. Las Casas surely gave his own life for the sake of his beloved, the oppressed Amerindian. Jesus Christ had hidden God in human flesh and blood. The relationship was there. Las Casas had the holiness of the Samaritan without knowing it or even seeking it. Because the victim was primary, the victimizers were primary. This is the classic behavior of those who appreciate the life of Jesus as much as they appreciate his death and resurrection, and who are concerned about the life of the world as much as its fall and redemption.

Las Casas also becomes a missioner for our time. We cannot present Christianity unless the scandal it has been involved in is resolved. The scandal is resolved by the reappearance of a true and selfless love for others. That will be only if there is a profound respect for the way the other has developed. That means knowledge of good and evil—but it is defined by the other as well as by Christianity. And it means appeal and the ability to be appealed to, so that a relationship appears, not a dictation. There can be no life to this relationship except a life of service. Neither wealth nor authority should be allowed to interrupt the relationship.

The features of the kingdom of God must be recognizable on earth or they will not be in heaven. The beauty of creation is the primary norm for reading God's purpose and for reading what has been made of that purpose by creatures themselves. The beauty of redemption then becomes a more passionate experience. That is primarily Jesus Christ. But it is Jesus Christ loosening the bonds of self-bound creatures, as they are socially and as they are singly. But for lack of Jesus in others, redemption is God unbinding creatures and freeing their original beauty in other ways. And for the lack of Jesus in others, redemption is God also unbinding creatures so they know whence the beauty of their being comes. Christian missioners live within the multiple redemptions made possible by God. They are willing to offer salvation in Jesus Christ on condition that others offer salvation in return in the name of their own beliefs. Missioners and missionized can live with what each has made of their own message until the restoration of creation through redeeming power whose love is stronger than death.

PART THREE

ON CHRISTOLOGY

CHAPTER 5

Christology and the Needs for Limits: The Contextualization of Theology

Lucien Richard

Interest in Christology is growing within the Roman Catholic context at a time when the central doctrine of the Incarnation is increasingly pressured to explain and justify itself (Hick, 1977). This pressure has led to very serious questioning: Did the doctrine of the Incarnation begin as an alien intrusion into Christianity? Is the Incarnation essential to Christian faith? According to M. Wiles, "the words 'Christianity' and 'Incarnation' are to many ears so nearly synonymous that the suggestion of a possible 'Christianity without Incarnation' will sound to them equally paradoxical and unintelligible" (Hick, 1977:1). Such a parallel is not the case, however, since Incarnation is an interpretation of the meaning and significance of Jesus, albeit a dominant interpretation:

> Incarnation, in its full and proper sense, is not something directly presented in scripture. It is a construction built on the variegated evidence to be found there. Increased historical knowledge has enabled our generation to see this truth about the way in which incarnational doctrine emerged more clearly than some earlier generations [Hick, 1977:7].

Not unrelated to these questions addressed to the symbol and doctrine of the Incarnation are a number of very strong reactions to any form of Christocentrism. These come specifically from those who are most concerned with the interreligious dialogue, which has been spelled out by Karl Rahner:

> Because of Jesus Christ, Christianity understands itself as the absolute religion, intended for all men, which cannot recognize any other religion beside itself as of equal right. . . . This pluralism is a greater threat and a

51

reason for greater unrest for Christianity than for any other religion. For no other religion—not even Islam—maintains so absolutely that it is THE religion, the one and only valid revelation of the one living God as does the Christian religion. The fact of the pluralism of religions, which endures and still from time to time becomes virulent and even after a history of 2000 years, must therefore be the greatest scandal and the greatest vexation for Christianity [Rahner, 118].

According to Paul Knitter and others, the stumbling block to any real dialogue with other religious traditions is "the central Christian belief in the uniqueness of Christ" (Knitter, 17).

Another demand for a revision of the church's position on Christ emerges from the perspective of liberation and political theology. Here one finds a movement toward theocentrism. According to Knitter:

Traditional Christology, with its insistence on finality and normativity, just does not fit what is being experienced in the arena of religious pluralism. We are in the midst of an evolution from Christocentrism to Theocentrism [Knitter, 166].

In light of this situation, it is my contention that the major task of contemporary theologians is to establish the boundaries, the limitations of Christology.

The Jesus of History and the Christ of Faith: The Limits of History and Faith

In the area of Christology, one basic principle has been operative from the very beginning: Christological maximalism; "more is better" or "too much is not enough." The principle unfolds in the following way: every possible importance that is not inconsistent with monotheism or with Jesus' specific humanity is to be ascribed to him. This maximalist principle follows from the central, although not undisputed, claim that Jesus Christ is the highest possible revelation of who God is. In qualifying the maximalist principle by inserting it into its monotheistic context and reaffirming the full humanity of Jesus, one is doing nothing different from what was done at Chalcedon. One is also setting certain boundaries, certain limitations. While these limitations are important and need to be addressed, my point of departure here is somewhat different. It is not, however, as we shall later see, as different as it would initially appear.

It is the application of the historical-critical method to the New Testament which furnishes us with the right elements to establish the boundaries, the limitations and constraints of Christology. It does so in various ways, but most specifically by establishing the real distinction between the Jesus of history and the Christ of faith. The major impact which the historical-critical method has had on theology and specifically on Christology was through its distinction of the historical Jesus and the Christ of faith. This distinction emphasized the role of history and that of experience in Christian faith. It underlined the fact that the articulation and formulation of Christian truth does not take place in a vacuum, but rather is realized within a historical and experiential process. Once this is admitted, Christianity acknowledges its dependence upon historical contingency in addition to God's revelation of the divine will and purposes. It is this dependence on history which alerts us to the discernment of what is true in religion, and leaves us puzzling about what belongs to God and what belongs to the vicissitudes of history and culture in the apprehension of religious truth.

The historical-critical method, in its emphasis both on history and experience, challenges one of the fundamental tenets of Christianity: the uniqueness and centrality of Jesus Christ and therefore the Christian's claim to truth. According to Peter Berger, the centrality of Christ forces theologians to devaluate the reality of history. The historical materials concerning Jesus as historical have no special position and therefore should be dealt with in the same way as other materials concerning other religious leaders.

> The questions I would then ask would be essentially the same as on any other record: What is being said here? What is the human experience out of which these statements come? And then: To what extent, and in what way, may we see here genuine discoveries of transcendent truth? [Berger, 105].[1]

To raise this distinction at all as something to be considered seriously is itself an indication of the climate within which theology must now be undertaken. It is to address that which was not an issue for generations for Protestant theologians before the Enlightenment and for Roman Catholic theologians until recent times. The basic debate arising from the distinction made between the Jesus of history and the Christ of faith is basically one about the relationship between the historical Jesus and Christian faith. It was this theological problem that lay behind Ernst Käsemann's decision to reopen the question of the historical Jesus (Käsemann, 15–47). For the basic question here, a question of who and what stood at the beginning of thematic Christology, not only bears on a matter of fact but also hinges upon a fact of great significance to Christianity as a religion in the minds of those who initiated the historical Jesus quests. The relation of Christological confessions to the Jesus of history, and indeed to his self-understanding, belongs inalienably to the center of Christianity. If Christology has no roots at all in the consciousness of the historical Jesus, how could it, in the end, vindicate its claim to be other than and much more than mere ideology? As is affirmed in the document *Select Questions on Christology*:

> Jesus Christ, the object-referent of the Church's faith, is neither a myth nor any sort of abstract notion. He is a man who lived in a concrete milieu, and who died after having lived his own life within the unfolding

of a historical process. It follows that historical research concerning Jesus Christ is demanded by the Christian faith itself [International Theological Commission, 1].

As an entrance into the issues I wish to address, the boundaries and limitations of Christology, I should like to quote Van Harvey. Referring to the problem of faith and history, he writes:

> [No problem] has caused more consternation and anxiety in the hearts and minds of Christian believers than the application of critical-historical methods to the New Testament, and especially to the life of Jesus. . . . My conviction is that . . . even the most sophisticated theological programs of the last two or three decades have failed to grapple in any rigorous and clear fashion with the thorny issues created by a revolution in the consciousness of Western man of which critical historiography is but the expression [V. Harvey, 11].

Although the critical-historical study of the New Testament begins with language and literary analysis, it cannot avoid the social-historical analysis of the context (ecclesial and other) of the text. This type of reading places distances between the text and the interpreter—between the text and Jesus. This distancing is the result of a historical consciousness where the socio-cultural embeddedness of all texts becomes a basic affirmation. Such embeddedness relativizes all texts, religious or others. Such distancing allows the community of faith to disengage itself from its past as well as from its present socio-cultural embeddedness and mistakes. According to Elizabeth Schüssler Fiorenza, the historical-critical method exercises a theological function (Schüssler Fiorenza, 12).[2]

By relativizing perspectives, interpretation simultaneously underlines the limitations and constraints that are the result of a historical conditioning.

The Constraints of History: Tradition

The constraints of history are basically the constraints of context; they are essentially those of time and space. Dietrich Bonhoeffer captured quite well the constraint of history by affirming that all historical events are "penultimate," that their ultimate significance lies in a reality that transcends them and transcends all the empirical coordinates of human existence. Few would dispute the observation that our contemporary understanding of history poses a fundamental challenge to traditional orthodox Christianity. That challenge is the challenge of the constraints of history on everything that touches human reality as human. The basic constraints are those of contexts as they affect human reality in its attempts to express itself. Such constraints can be understood as tradition.

In Romans 10:13–15, Paul outlines the basic process that governs access to

Christian existence: "everyone who invokes the name of the Lord will be saved." And how could they invoke one in whom they had no faith? And how could they have faith in one they had never heard of? And how could they hear without someone to spread the news? And how could someone spread the news without a commission to do so? And that is what scripture clearly affirms: "How welcome are the feet of the messengers of good news!" Faith in Christ, and therefore Christian existence, is essentially ecclesial. It is as recipient of the gospel that the church is church. It is in connection with the church that later generations have access to the revelation of God in Jesus Christ. Accepting Ernest Troeltsch's important insight, David Tracy writes: "It is the tradition of the church that is our central mediation to the actual Jesus—the Jesus remembered by the church; it is our present experience of the mediated Christ-event which impels our belief in Jesus Christ" (Tracy, 322).

The present experience of the Christ-event is mediated through tradition. Trust in the reality of the Christ-event as made present to us implies essentially trust in the mediation itself (Tracy, 323). According to Edward Schillebeeckx, at the origin of Christology lies an experience—that final salvation from God is disclosed in the person of Jesus. That person brought to life a movement, and it is through this movement that we are confronted here and now with Jesus the Christ. The movement which Jesus set afoot remains the medium for any approach to Jesus the Christ. "The only knowledge we possess of the Christ event reaches us via the concrete experience of the first local communities of Christians who were sensitive of a new life present in them" (Schillebeeckx, 47). The Christological titles are an attempt on the part of the early church to express in words their past and present experience of Jesus. While the titles, according to Schillebeeckx, are important, they are relative to the communal experience; for what is essential is the Christian experience of the local church. The saving experience persists and from time to time calls for an appropriate expression and articulation in new social and historical situations" (Schillebeeckx, 46).

The proto-Christian movement centered around Jesus is the inescapable and historically reliable point of departure. In keeping with his principle that the norm and criterion of any interpretation of Jesus of Nazareth is Jesus of Nazareth himself (Schillebeeckx, 43–76), Schillebeeckx combines the recognition that "the question about the unique and universal significance of Jesus is one that can only be answered in terms of belief" with insistence that such faith must have a solid basis in Jesus' life history. "If the Christian affirmation of Jesus' universal significance is not ideological but is an assent to reality, something in the record of Jesus must point in that direction. . . . In the historical man Jesus there must be present some ground or reason for our being able to acknowledge him in that way" (Schillebeeckx, 604). Historical foundation of this sort is indispensable in Christology, Schillebeeckx maintains, unless one holds that Jesus, whatever the facts of his life may have been, is simply made into a representative symbol of human aspirations by the subsequent activity of others who profess faith in him.

The Christ-event is mediated through the particular historical form that the Christian church is. Thus, the church as tradition is the way for the organization of human experience as Christian. This systematic organization is a communal possession, which provides stability and an effective way of living for the believer. As Christians, individuals are socialized and constituted by the Christian tradition. It is the Christian tradition which enables the individual to remember the past Christ-event, celebrate its actual presence and anticipate its future fulfillment. Tradition plays an integrating role by uniting past, present, and future. Ecclesial communities are, therefore, in Gaislain LaFont's words:

> At once theological place and hermeneutical place. They are the former because if the conduct and the objectives which define a community are in conformity with the Gospel in a given situation they deliver by themselves something of the evangelical message which can be read and revealed only there. They are a hermeneutical place because the objective gift of faith is never perceived except from the angle from which each of the communities, in fact, receives and lives it [LaFont, 4].

As such, within the Christian context, theology is essentially an ecclesial discipline; it can be done only within a believing community. As an ecclesial discipline, theology is essentially hermeneutical. It begins neither with a set of a prioris, whether philosophical or dogmatic, nor with an unmediated experience. It begins with a collective memory lived and handed down in an ecclesial community. In a hermeneutical theology, understanding can never be the product of the individual's autobiographical reflection alone. Inherited knowledge constitutes the framework in which an individual perceives an experience.

A decision of faith which does not find any point of contact in human experience is irrational. God's transcendence is not such that it never touches human existence. The historical-critical approach to the New Testament made us aware of the cultural and therefore relative nature of the text, but it also demonstrated that the tradition within which these texts originated is a living tradition, a community of faith. Within that living tradition the disclosive and revelatory function of Jesus Christ is not located simply in the past but also in the present. The writers of the New Testament can exercise freedom with respect to the Jesus traditions because they believe that the Jesus who spoke in the past is the same Jesus who now speaks to his followers through the Holy Spirit.

Revelation is not located simply in the past but in actual community. This fact has implications for every generation of Christians in its relation to the past event. It also has implications for the understanding of revelation and its relation to actual Christian experience. The historical-critical method poses the basic question about the relation between the fact of the historical Jesus and the fact of the church's faith; the fact of history and the fact of experience.

Both facts are determined by the limitations and constraints of history and culture, albeit in different ways.

The emphasis given to tradition, to actual experience, and to the historical fact of Jesus provides the context for the basic question about the limits and constraints in Christology. Both the historical and the experiential are social and cultural realities. Any Christological construct is enabled and controlled by sociological conditions of context, transmission, and plausibility. The social construction of reality implies that persons and groups build institutions. They form a social reality which persons encounter. They constitute society as objective reality, whereas objective reality refers to life as it is institutionally defined. Society as "subjective reality" is reality as apprehended in individual consciousness. Subjective reality develops via the acquisition of an identity through socialization.

The inherited Christian tradition forms the Christian individual's identity. Christian identity is thus the result of a process of socialization. Socialization involves the process of being inserted into a socio-cultural environment which in fact produces one's self-identity. That process of insertion demands the internalization of the society's self-understanding, self-image, and valuing. Thomas Groome, paraphrasing Herbert Mead, writes:

> Having externalized ourselves into culture and society, and culture and society having taken on a life of their own, the empowerments and limitations of that world are now taken back into our consciousness as our own. The possibilities and parameters that our social/cultural context appears to offer become our own perception of our possibilities and parameters. In other words, the objectified culture and society created by us and our predecessors become internalized as the basis of our own self-identity [Groome, 112].

The process of socialization determines the process of self-interpretation. As Joseph Cahill writes: "in many instances this self-interpretation is really a misnomer since the interpretation is really done by others rather than by a genuinely autonomous or inner-directed self" (Cahill, 154).

Within the process of the Christian tradition, socialization and self-interpretation imply the inter-relation of the historical and the experiential. This sets up the basic hermeneutical problem in Christology. The problem then, is, first and foremost, the existence of a critical tension between the Jesus event, his person, message, ministry, and death, and the Christ-event. This latter event can be understood as relating to the aspirations and ideologies present in the cultural environment of the early church who first confessed Jesus to be Lord and by extension to the relation of both the Jesus-event and Christ-event as these relate to our culture. This tension explains the diversity of the numerous Christological responses. Tension is created in the attempt to relate history, experience, and the Christian fact, which is understood as revelatory and disclosive of the transcendent in our midst. It is this revelatory-disclosive nature of the Christian fact which makes possible a Christian religious experience, a faith experience.

As experience, Christian faith is the crossing of a boundary within the dimensions of human existence. The particular fact of experience that forms the Christian faith is not only dependent upon the offer of the reality itself (God in Jesus Christ) but also upon tradition as expressed in texts, creeds, liturgy. Therefore it is inherently colored by what is technically described as the cultural context. This implies that what is reality for faith is set in the midst of history, and is itself an intrinsic part of human life. History is itself history and therefore cultural. Revelation and the cultural, communal, historical expression of it are not to be had separately. Revelation is always partly given in what Paul Ricoeur calls *le croyable disponible*, plausible structures of a certain period—that is to say that the whole is formed by generally accepted assumptions, expectations, and ideologies.

The Limits and Limitations of Culture

The revelation offered to us in Jesus Christ cannot remain outside human life and experience. The gift of revelation is not given either from above or from below, but horizontally in the encounter of human beings with one another, within our human history. According to Schillebeeckx, this is affirmed in the fact that revelation in Jesus Christ comes to us in and through human language. As such it includes an interpretive dimension and must take place within the context of cultural history and thus remain embedded in a specific cultural tradition.

Ultimately and formally, the limits of Christology as the systematic expression in language of the disclosive and revelatory nature of Jesus' life, ministry, death and resurrection must be found in the limitations and constraints of culture itself. But culture is understood in a variety of ways, which affect the nature of its limiting and constraining functions. Different approaches to anthropology, sociology, and history lead to different understandings of culture.

As in every other organized field of knowledge anthropology, sociology, and history have their own metaphors, models, and paradigms. Two basic metaphors have governed the above-mentioned fields—the mechanical and the organic. In the mechanical metaphor, machines serve for the understanding of human behavior. Human beings are often referred to as complex robots—computers. Epistemologically, when mechanical metaphors are used to describe culture, the principle of analysis is used. The concept "machine" implies putting together a number of parts in an organized and functioning way. The finished product is not greater than the sum of its parts, and can be decomposed into its components. As such it can be analyzed and understood. This approach to human behavior and to culture is basically reductionist. The person is considered as a self-contained individualistic reality. When the principle of analysis is applied to persons and cultures, it is understood that the manipulation, prediction, and control of component parts are real explanation.

As Edmund Sullivan writes: "explanation of a phenomenon involves an attempt to manipulate, control and predict antecedent, consequent conditions with a view to refining linear causality" (Sullivan, 5). Within this understanding, causality is simply the relationship between antecedent conditions and consequences. What we have here is complete psychological and social determinism. In this perspective, limits and constraints are understood in a materialistic way; there is little place for change except through manipulation and the application of techniques. In the mechanical mode of intelligibility there is an assumption that human action or behavior can be understood when a causal relation can be grasped between a specific behavior and various antecedent conditions. Here human action can be understood in relation to its more simple components. While the mechanical metaphor originates in physical systems, the organic metaphor is premised on biological systems—on a living organism not on a machine. An organism is a living and adaptive reality which can change itself as it relates dynamically to its environment. Here a totality is more than its parts, and the process of knowing is through synthesis, not analysis. There is a preoccupation with structural totalities characterized by internal dependencies. Structures are characterized by multiple transformations interdependent with each other. In this model, limits and constraints are understood not deterministically but in a vital way. Change can occur, not simply by manipulation but from interaction. Intelligibility within this framework is teleological—that is, in terms of goals attained. Sullivan writes: "The important point to be made about all these cases is that the understanding of a phenomenon is not primarily in terms of the demonstration of causal sequence, but in the articulation of the form or structure that generates phenomena" (content) (Sullivan, 37). Yet this intelligibility undervalues the importance of the role of conscious intentions of human agents.

John MacMurray, who developed a personal metaphor for culture, has this to say about the organic metaphor:

> We are not organisms, but persons. The nexus of relations which unites us in a human society is not organic but personal. Human behavior cannot be understood, but only caricatured, if it is represented as an adaptation to environment; and there is no such process as social evolution but, instead, a history which reveals a precarious development and possibilities both of progress and of retrogression. . . . The personal necessarily includes an organic aspect . . . and this organic aspect is continuously qualified by its conclusion, so that it cannot even be properly abstracted, except through a prior understanding of the personal structure in which it is an essential, though subordinate, component. A descent from the personal is possible, in theory, and indeed in practice; but there is no way to ascend from the organic to the personal. The organic conception of man excludes, by its very nature, all the characteristics in virtue of which we are human beings. To include them we must change our categories afresh from the beginning [MacMurray, 46–47].

Sullivan has applied this metaphor to the cultural world. A personal metaphor attempts to incorporate the conscious intentions of agents as part of the interpretive practice (Sullivan, 15). It is built upon the assumption that human language is an essential and irreducible element in our understanding of humans (Sahlens, 61).[3] Since language assumes reciprocity, one can say that the unit of analysis is not an individual actor or nomad but rather a relationship of dialogue. In other words, the unit of analysis is totality (I-Thou) that cannot be broken down further without losing the core metaphor of communication. Emphasis on language reveals the importance of the relational quality of the personal world without denying the importance of the subject and his or her consciousness. The position developed is primarily focused on language and its cultural function.

With the preeminence of language, communication becomes an essential feature and element of this metaphor. MacMurray writes:

> Speech is public. It is at once thought and action, or rather a unity of which "mental" and "physical" activity are distinguishable but inseparable aspects; and as a result it establishes communication, and introduces the "you" as a correlative of the "I." For if this "I think" logically excludes the second person, the "I say" is logically incomplete. To complete it we must formulate it as follows: "I say to you, and I await your response." Thus the problem of the form of the personal emerges as the problem of the form of communication [MacMurray, 74].

Within that framework, individual expressions or symbols are for purposes of communication. The assumption is that individuals use expressions because they intend meanings for others. Expressions are ambiguous because their meaning is contingent upon the communication of many actors with one another. Humans are involved in webs of significance that they themselves have spun. The personal world is the cultural world; culture is the womb in which personhood grows and is transformed—and, in its turn, transforms. The personal world is cultivated within cultural forms.

One of the fundamental assumptions of this point of view is that human behavior is understandable only in terms of a dynamic social reference. Culture always exists as a web of dynamic social relations. According to Sullivan: "The analysis of culture, which is the pole of the personal world, is set off and polarized with the structural dimensions of class structure, gender, race, and so on" (Sullivan, 25). A personal metaphor for culture demands a personal mode of interpretation. Personal interpretation tries to understand the person as an active agent whose expressions are for others. Such a metaphor also implies that the intentional self is not only the receiver of cultural constraints, but also a transformer of such constraints.

The word "constraint" as employed here is meaningful in the context of an understanding of culture where language and communication are primary. Within that same understanding, the concept of limitation takes on another meaning. Historical and social realities can always be analyzed in terms of their relation to a particular "compound of limitations." Such compounds are constituted by a variety of different kinds of limitations. Limitations can be continuous, contextual, or contingent-continuous, such as the structure of physiology or the unforseeability of the future; contextual, such as time and place; or contingent, as basically related to an individual's taste. If we wish to arrive at as full an understanding as possible of any manifest cultural phenomenon, it is necessary to specify, as exactly as possible, the whole compound of limitations which has constrained the phenomenon into its particular observable form. This involves an analysis both of the limitations toward which it is directed and of the limitations which have controlled and constrained the attainment of that direction.

The word "constraint" as used here is understood from within our understanding of culture. Rather than looking at an item in isolation as a kind of inevitable fact and then looking for immediate antecedents which might be explanatory of that fact, it is far more illuminating to look at the whole range or repertory of possible eventualities and then to ask what has constrained this particular item into its actual expression.

This approach admits the adequate integration of a social and conscious component. It supplies the context of explanation, the frame within which explanation can occur, but without which explanation is improbable. The process includes within itself an individual component. In fact the reason for referring to "compounds of limitation" and not simply "constraint" is to include the highly important component of consciousness. For human beings are not simply constrained. Through consciousness there is the possibility to discern the limitations and often to move on, to bring about newness. Provided that we keep a prior and very steady eye on the notion of limitation, we will find that the interaction of the social and the individual becomes much easier to handle because the focal point of analytic reference lies outside a decision about the priority of the individual or the social in absolute terms. This concept of limitation and constraints, inserted within a personal understanding of the structure of culture and its laws, has been applied to Christology by scholars in various fields.

Christology and the Constraints of History

According to A. E. Harvey, Jesus as a communicator had to recognize the constraints of his listeners: "He had to speak a language they could understand, perform actions they would find intelligible, and conduct his life and undergo his death in a manner of which they could make some sense" (Harvey, 7). According to Harvey, modern research has made available a great deal of material about the first century and has enabled us to find a new precision to the study of the constraints to which Jesus was exposed. Harvey applies this understanding to the scriptural affirmation that Jesus was a teacher. Biographical affirmations which seem to have little relevance to basic Christological questions, when seen in light of the kinds of limitations and constraints described above, take on valuable significance:

> The statement, for example, that Jesus was a teacher, when set in the context of the constraints which bore upon any teacher of his time and culture and of the relatively small number of options which were open to anyone who wished to give a new lead in religious understanding while remaining intelligible to the majority of his hearers—such a statement is capable of yielding a surprising amount of information about the kind of person Jesus must have been and the kind of achievement at which he aimed; and this information is of great relevance to the ultimate question of Christology: who and what was Jesus [A. Harvey, 7].[4]

Theologians and exegetes have made the point that the type of information they need in order to move beyond certain historical affirmations about Jesus into the Christological area is simply not available in the scriptural sources. Theologians, when seeking to formulate the doctrines of the Incarnation, have looked to the gospels, not for the bare bones of Jesus' biography, but for information about such subtle and intimate matters as his so-called messianic consciousness, his moral perfection, or his relationship with his heavenly father. Yet it became evident that anything which purported to be an answer to the theologian's question can be shown to be itself the product of theological reflection in the early church and to offer little access to the mind of Jesus.

Treated as historical documents, as they now must be, the gospels can offer us secure information only of a factual historical kind. To pursue such matters as a doctrine of the person of Christ, theologians have to draw conclusions from premises established elsewhere. Writing about the sinlessness of Jesus, an affirmation with a great deal of theological implications, Dennis Nineham states:

> Is it, however, possible to validate claims of the kind in question on the basis of historical evidence? To prove an historical negative, such as the sinlessness of Jesus, is notoriously difficult to the point of impossibility. How, for example, could even the most constant companion of Jesus have been sure that he remained unbrokenly true to his own principles and never, for example, "looked on a woman to lust after her" in the sense of Matthew 5:28? Such a question is not for a moment asked with any intention of casting doubt on the sexual purity of Jesus; it is meant simply as an example designed to show that the sort of claims for Jesus we are discussing could not be justified to the hilt by any historical records, however full or intimate or contemporary they might be, and even if their primary concern was with the quality and development of Jesus' inner life and character [Nineham, 188].

Systematic theologians therefore find themselves in a dilemma; although they do not wish to disengage themselves from historical questions that inevitably arise concerning the question of the proper interpretation of Jesus of Nazareth, they do not wish to be trapped by them. According to H. J. Cadbury, the Gospels do not give us enough evidence to guarantee the self-consistency of Jesus:

> Certainly one cannot dissociate a man from his teaching, and if Jesus' distinctive teachings were reinforced by his own practice the total impression would be enhanced. Christians assume that this was the case, but apart from his teachings, unambiguous evidence on the character of Jesus is somewhat scanty. The teachings themselves have a certain unity of suggestion, but they are not point by point confirmed by examples of Jesus' own conformity to them [Nineham, 188].

A. E. Harvey and E. P. Sanders in their approach to the New Testament, do not concentrate on the teachings of Jesus, but on the fact that Jesus was known to be a teacher. That fact must be understood within its cultural context, culture being understood within the framework of a personal metaphor. Such a fact (being a teacher) must be understood in its limitations and constraints. Here there is no collapsing of fact into interpretation, and yet because of the constraints and limitations upon a historical fact, there are no facts without important information about the historical actors. Facts as human facts are expressive, communicative. Subjective feelings and states are not the only aspects of experience that can be trusted and that really matter. The personal agent does not exist in a no-man's-land of free-floating interpersonal relationships. As R. Jacoby writes: "The individual before it can determine itself is determined by the relations in which it is enmeshed. It is a fellow-being before it's a being" (Jacoby, 18).

A human fact is not simply intelligible from the point of view of the agent, but is also dependent upon the interpretive schema of those who receive the expression to understand. Motives or intentions are a constitutive part of human action and therefore of human fact. Within the limits of constraint, human behavior is determined by the motivation of the actor. Human agents not only act but also undergo action that is partly out of their control. The meaning or significance of a human act is the place that it occupies in a network of relationships.

It tended to be almost a taboo question in many circles to ask what Jesus was up to. Sanders and A. E. Harvey seem less fearful on this point. Harvey affirms that "the evidence for at least the main facts of the life and death of Jesus is as abundant, circumstantial and consistent as is the case with any other figure of ancient history" (A. Harvey, 5–6). Those facts, which would seem to be of little relevance for the theologian, when submitted to the technique of constraint and limitations, emerge as theologically valuable.

The Christain Claim of the Uniquesness of Christ
and the Constraints of Experience

Within our basic understanding of human existence as personal and essentially social, experience has to do with receptiveness toward the real in all its dimensions. Experience bridges the objective and subjective. There is no such thing as pure subjectivity. The Kantian transcendental analysis of human subjectivity has been shown to be inadequate. Human subjectivity is always historically conditioned. Persons stand within the history of a tradition of ideas and values.

Since we are essentially linguistic beings, speech is an ingredient of experience. This implies that our own experience emerges from within a context where reality has already been interpreted and brought to language. The subject who experiences is in reality also part of existing society and not an abstract individual.

While experience and consciousness are not synonymous, they are intimately linked. Consciousness is the experience of separation and limitation over and against others and nature. Both consciousness and experience must be seen in a relational totality. As R. M. Unger writes:

Consciousness implies autonomous identity, the experience of division from other selves. But the medium through which consciousness expresses itself is made up of the symbols of culture, and these, according to the principle of totality, are irreducibly social. When you speak of language or make a gesture, you perceive and communicate meaning in categories that are the common patrimony of many men. By what power can you and they speak to one another? It must be possible for each to view the other's statements and acts as the signs of certain intentions. These intentions can, in turn, be understood because they are intentions you too might have. It follows that consciousness always presupposes the possibility of viewing other persons as selves that could, under favorable enough circumstances, see what one sees and believe what one believes. That is the cognitive aspect of sociability [Unger, 215].

The personal mode, and therefore interpersonal mode, of experience and consciousness challenges the notion of a transcendental consciousness and experience. Consciousness and experience can never come into existence or find expression except in terms of a social environment. The socio-cultural environment emphasizes the situated character of conscious and intentional action.

The conditioning of human consciousness and experience by culture and tradition challenges the notion of a transcendental analysis of the religiously revelatory and disclosive nature of human consciousness and experience. There is no consciousness, no experience of the religious and therefore revelatory dimension of reality, that can escape historical and cultural conditioning.

The metaphor of the personal assumes a concept of culture within its reality. The personal world is a cultural world. Culture is like a second nature. As Sullivan writes:

> The contention is that the personal world and all its relationships are embedded in a specific history with all of the idiosyncrasies and limitations entailed therein. The personal world is, therefore, a real historical event rather than some abstract formulation of an ideal person. Therefore, when we speak of a personal world, we are essentially talking about an identifiable located cultural form. The essence of that form is constitutive relationships—that is, the particular way a social group is connected to the objects, artifacts, institutions, and systematic practices of those that surround it [Sullivan, 72].

The personal world as a located cultural world forms a dynamic totality; and as such, it is a set of relations embedded in material-historical realities.

It is quite clear that the earliest Christians could hardly have occupied themselves with the question posed by later theologians: whether, and in what sense, Jesus was God. As Jews they were severely and passionately monotheist, professing a monotheism explicitly accepted by Jesus himself. The first community, in order to affirm that Jesus was more than one of the prophets—that his authority had a certain finality or absoluteness about it not found in others—had few options left to it but to tell the story of Jesus in such a way that his authority would become apparent and would confront other hearers, as it had confronted those who had witnessed it, with the necessity to make up their minds—to declare themselves for or against Jesus. Seen from this perspective of limitations and constraints, the kind of information available about Jesus from the gospels no longer appears irrelevant to Christology.

The constraints of history and of culture are not such that the historical fact of Jesus becomes insignificant and of no value to the contemporary Christian. But the historical Jesus is only one pole of the contemporary Christian fact. The other pole is the Christ of faith—that is, the disclosive nature of Jesus' life, ministry, death and resurrection, and the faith response of the early Christians and of contemporary Christians. According to Wilfred Cantwell Smith, history can provide a context large enough to include both the objective findings of the scientific historical study of the scriptures and one's deep personal experience of a religious tradition (Smith, 1981). Yet the question arises: Can such an historical perspective avoid a form of reductionism? Can historical scholarship allow for the full, even naive, experience of one's religious tradition as disclosive or even revelatory? This understanding seems to conflict with perspectives that emerge from the historical understanding of the gospels. A particularly interesting example of this is given by John Hick. He argues that difference in religion is essentially due to cultural provenance:

> This means that it is not appropriate to speak of a religion as being true or false. . . . For the religions, in the sense of distinguishable religio-

cultural streams within man's history, are expressions of the diversities of human types and temperaments and thought forms. This did not come about because religious reality required this, but because such a development was historically inevitable in the days of undeveloped communication between the cultural groups. But now that the world has become a communicational unity, we are moving into a new situation in which it becomes both possible and appropriate for religious thinking to transcend these cultural-historical boundaries [Hick, 1973:124].

As faiths meet and interact they are likely to arrive at some form of intellectual unity. The greatest difficulty we face is the nature of the central revelatory symbol in Christianity, Jesus the Christ, as unique and absolute. According to Hick, Christian thinkers have a clear responsibility to find ways to departicularize the Christ. From an historical perspective the problem arises that we do not have enough comparative material to allow an absolute judgment about uniqueness. History, in fact, has grave difficulty with the category "unique." Adequate comparative information is never available to permit such judgments as "uniquely good," "uniquely compassionate," and the like. To use such language is to shift from the perspective of critical history to that of faith, of revelation and disclosure. The question arises again about limitations and constraints, not simply about history but also about human experience.

According to Van Harvey, in the area of critical history the principle of analogy entails a conception of facts as closed in principle to any special revelatory act of God. The fact of Christianity is the fact of a people who found salvation "from God" in Jesus of Nazareth. Christians found it in such a radical way that we can speak of discovery about revelation and this from *the particular*, from that which is historically situated and determined. Within the Christian movement, the saving experience persists and from time to time calls for an appropriate expression and articulation in different social and historical situations. Schillebeeckx writes:

One might call it a "disclosure" experience, a discovery event: a source experience (both for the person who had known Jesus directly and for the one who had come to know about him by way of the MEMORIA JESU and the life of the local congregation); that is to say, they have discovered in Jesus something that cannot be pinned down directly, on an empirical basis, but that to any open-minded person confronted with Jesus in a living community is going to present itself as something gratuitous, as "given in evidence" [Schillebeeckx, 57].

The fact of the Christian movement with its explicit reference to Jesus poses the basic question of religious experience. The question is not simply about the possibility of experiencing theistically in a subjective manner, but rather about experiencing as corresponding to reality external to the human projection. The fact of the Christian movement poses the question about the discovery, the possible discovery, of God. The corporate belief of a community seems to provide the necessary matrix for the emergence of personal creeds that appear to the individual as something totally different. While the possibilities and parameters intrinsic to tradition tend to become the individual's own, the individual is not ultimately determined by the socialization process. Change can occur; individuals can be critical and need to be critical of their cultural/ social structures.

Within a "personal" understanding of culture, there is always the possibility of uniqueness and resistance to that culture. The personal self is not only the receiver of cultural constraints, it is also a transformer of the institutions that shape it. Yet the experience of something new and surprising is always an experience of the familiar. Discovering something new is also a rediscovery. The new is never radically the "wholly other," for the simple reason that in our experiences we ourselves are part of this reality which reveals itself to us. Reality has already revealed itself, albeit in such a way that we recognize this revelation only as something that is already familiar to us. Our experiences are neither purely objective nor purely subjective. At least partially, there is something that is "given," which we cannot completely manipulate or change. Yet experience implies personal involvement with its reminiscences and sensibilities. Thus, the irreducible elements of our experiences form a totality which already contains interpretation. In the act of interpreting, we experience without being able to draw a neat distinction between the element of experience and the element of interpretation. There is no experience without "theorizing."

The fact of the possibility of personal experience of thought and consciousness implies that a human being is an intentional being—a construing being. Future is part of experience. The personal world is not only governed by the past but is also projected into a future. The notion of "project" expresses the importance of the intentional futurity of human action. Nevertheless, reality remains the final criterion; it can destroy all our projects. Through such resistance of reality, we come into contact with a reality which is independent of us—not thought of, made, or projected by men and women. As Schillebeeckx writes:

> At this point we have a revelation of that which cannot be manipulated, a "transcendent" power, something that comes "from elsewhere," which asserts its validity in the face of our projects and nevertheless makes all human plans, products and considerations possible, by virtue of its critical and negative orientation [Schillebeeckx, 34].

Surprisingly unexpected new ways of perceiving are opened in and through the resistance presented by reality. The permanent resistance of reality to our rational inventions forces us to continually new and untried models of thought:

> The hermeneutical principle for the disclosure of reality is not the self-evident, but the scandal, the stumbling block of the refractoriness of

reality. Reality is always a surprising revelation for thought, for which thought can only be a witness. In such experiences of what proves completely refractory to all our inventions we shall finally also discover the basis for what we rightly call revelation " [Schillebeeckx, 34].

There is always otherness being encountered, otherness always ahead. Religious experience is experience of human life in the world, but experienced as an encounter and in this respect as a disclosure of God. Revelation takes place in historical human experiences in the world but at the same time it summons us from what we take for granted in our limited world. It is therefore not to be found in any direct appeal to our so-called self-evident experiences within the world. As experience it is the crossing of a boundary within the dimensions of human existence.

To establish the truth of the religious tradition that led to Christology, one needs to measure this tradition and its language against the whole of our experience of reality. The whole of reality is historical process which remains incomplete. The truth of Christology is above all a question of the concretion of personal and cultural existence. Within this context, the concept of relativity is not a substitute for, but rather a critical assessment of, universalism. What is affirmed at Chalcedon is that the immanence of God in no way destroys the integrity of history.

In Christology, the constraints of history and experience must lead us to a spirit of patient induction and an attitude of openness to the fullness of human experience. History and experience in their own facticity remain ambiguous. It is not possible for us to reach out in advance to a Christological affirmation about our human reality that is not essentially eschatological.

Notes

1. The author continues with the following: "Much has been made in recent Protestant theology of the centralness of Christ and the alleged necessity of starting the theological enterprise with the figure of Christ. At its worst, this approach systematizes the rape of the historical materials, as when Christian beliefs are read back into the religious history of ancient Israel. But even at its most sophisticated, when history is treated carefully and respectfully, it means that all theological interpretations of historical materials should emanate from this one central focus, which is itself taken as an unchanging a priori. I repudiate such a procedure. I would take the historical materials concerning Christ, both the New Testament itself and the subsequent literature, as a record of a specific complex of human experience. As such, it has no special position as against any comparable record (say, the record concerning the Buddha in the Pali canon and the subsequent ramifications of Buddhist thought)."

2. The author writes: "1. It asserts the meaning of the original witness over and against later dogmatic and societal usurpations, for different purposes. 2. It makes the assimilation of the text to our own experience, parochial pietism, and church-interests, more difficult. 3. It keeps alive the 'irritation' of the original text by

challenging our own assumptions, world view, and practice. 4. It limits the number of interpretations which can be given to a text. The 'spiritual' meanings of biblical text are limited by its literal-historical meanings."

3. M.D. Sahlens writes: " . . . if we were to disregard language, culture would differ from animal tradition only in degree. But precisely because [of] this involvement with language—a phrase hardly befitting serious scientific discourse—cultural–social life differs from the animal in kind. It is not just the expression of an animal of another kind. The reason why human social behavior is not organized by the individual maximization of genetic interest is that human beings are not socially defined by organic qualities but in terms of symbolic attributes; and a symbol is precisely a meaningful value such as 'close kinship' or 'shared blood'—which cannot be determined by the physical properties of that to which it refers."

4. The author continues: "These constraints in turn allow us to establish the options which were open to a person such as we believe Jesus to have been, and give objective content to those general statements about him which we regard as historically established. In this way we can begin to build up a profile of Jesus which is independent of Christian sources and which offers some kind of test by which the reliability of these sources can be checked."

References

Berger, Peter. 1969. *Rumor of Angels*. Garden City, NY: Doubleday.

Cahill, Joseph. 1982. *Mended Speech: The Crisis of Religious Studies and Theology*. New York: Crossroad.

Douglas, Mary. 1970. *Natural Symbols*. New York: Pantheon.

Groome, Thomas. 1980. *Christian Religious Education*. San Francisco: Harper and Row.

Harvey, A. E. 1982. *Jesus and the Constraints of History*. Philadelphia: Westminster.

Harvey, Van A. 1969. *The Historian and the Believer*. New York: Macmillan.

Hick, John. 1973. *Philosophy of Religion*. Englewood Cliffs, NJ: Prentice Hall.

———, ed. 1977. *The Myth of God Incarnate*. Philadelphia: Westminster.

International Theological Commission. 1980. *Select Questions on Christology*. Washington, DC: USCC.

Jacoby, R. 1975. *Social Amnesia*. Boston: Beacon.

Käsemann, Ernst. 1964. "The Problem of the Historical Jesus," in *Essays on New Testament Themes*. London: SCM.

Knitter, Paul. 1985. *No Other Name? A Critical Survey of Christian Attitudes Toward the World Religions*. Maryknoll, NY: Orbis.

LaFont, Gaislain. 1976. "Monastic Life and Theological Studies," in *Monastic Studies*, vol. 12.

MacMurray, John. 1961. *Persons in Relation*. London: Farber and Farber.

Nineham, Dennis. 1977. *The Myth of God Incarnate*. Garden City, NY: Doubleday.

Rahner, Karl. 1966. "Christianity and the Non-Christian Religions," in *Theological Investigations*, vol. 5. Baltimore: Helicon.

Sahlens, M. D. 1976. *The Use and Abuse of Biology*. Ann Arbor: University of Michigan Press.

Sanders, E. P. 1985. *Jesus and Judaism*. Philadelphia: Fortress.

Schillebeeckx, Edward. 1979. *Jesus: An Experiment in Christology*. New York: Crossroad.

Schüssler Fiorenza, Elizabeth. 1984. "Contemporary Biblical Scholarship: Its Directions," in Francis Igo, ed. *Modern Biblical Scholarship: Its Impact on Theology and Proclamation.* Villanova: Villanova University Press.

Smith, Wilfred Cantwell. 1981. *Towards a World Theology.* Philadelphia: Westminster.

Sullivan, Edmond. 1984. *A Critical Psychology: Interpretation of the Personal World.* New York: Plenum.

Tracy, David. 1981. *The Analogical Imagination.* New York: Crossroad.

Unger, R. M. 1975. *Knowledge and Politics.* New York: Free Press.

CHAPTER 6

A Feminist Christological Exploration

Barbara Darling-Smith

Theology, rational reflection on the faith, is done by particular individuals with particular histories and in particular communities. I will tell you, then, a bit of my history. I was raised in an evangelical Protestant home and church. One of the most emphasized teachings of the tradition in which I grew up was that one's faith made a difference in one's life. This firm conviction, which I accepted in my childhood and continue to affirm, is shared with liberation theologies in general and feminist theology in particular, with which I identify myself as an adult. At the same time I continue to identify myself as a Christian—although now within the mainline Protestant tradition. Faith can, of course, make a difference only if it is integrally related to our life and experience—our context. As Christians we are called to relate our faith to the contemporary events which shape our lives.

One such event is the struggle for liberation being waged by people of color, by the poor around the globe, and by women of all races. Often this passionate commitment to justice and liberation has arisen directly out of people's Christian faith. Liberation theologians often use scripture as a prophetic critique of oppression, pointing to God's "preferential option for the poor" and proclaiming God as the "God of the oppressed" (see Cone, 1975). They utilize the prophetic cries for social justice and cite Jesus' ministry to the poor, the oppressed, and the outcast (see, for example, Luke 4:16–30).

Yet, as Elisabeth Schüssler Fiorenza has pointed out, a crucial conflict arises between this liberationist appropriation of the Christian message and the claim of many feminists that the Bible and Christian tradition are sexist and have sanctioned and encouraged the oppression of women (Schüssler Fiorenza, 52).

It cannot be denied that the church has often oppressed women. The feminist literature cites many examples of denials of women's full humanity. For twenty centuries church leadership has been overwhelmingly male, and women have been admonished to listen to the wise counsel of men.

One obvious and powerful factor in the way the church has devalued women is the predominating use of male imagery for the divine. The Trinity is God the Father, God the Son, and God the Holy Spirit. The message is clear to men and women alike: maleness is closer to the divine than is femaleness, and is thus normative humanness. This message comes from the Christian faith's affirmation that Jesus of Nazareth, a male human being, is the Christ, God incarnate, who plays a unique role in reconciling humanity to God. In a hypothetical world where women and men were completely equal it would make no difference whether the savior figure were male or female. Yet set within the context of a culture where men possess the power (every culture from Greco-Roman times up through our own), this male savior figure gave the church—whose leadership was increasingly made up of men—sanction for its claims that men were closer physically to Jesus, the Savior, and therefore better able to represent him. The church has combined the doctrine of Jesus the Christ as savior figure with the fact of Jesus' maleness, thus devaluing women. Mary Daly has pointed out:

> The idea of a unique male savior . . . [is] one more legitimation of male superiority. Indeed, there is reason to see it as a perpetuation of patriarchal religion's "original sin" of servitude to patriarchy itself. . . . Such a symbol lends itself to reinforcement of the prevailing hierarchies. Under the conditions of patriarchy the role of liberating the human race from the original sin of sexism would seem to be precisely the role that a male symbol cannot perform. . . . The image itself is one-sided, as far as sexual identity is concerned, and it is precisely on the wrong side, since it fails to counter sexism and functions to glorify maleness [Daly, 71–72].

Recognizing the damaging effects on women's self-esteem and powers of self-affirmation, many women have decided that the church is unable to be a redemptive community for them. They have left the Christian faith entirely to join feminist communities of spirituality, which find the divine in the Goddess symbol and in themselves.

This courageous move—to leave the church and refuse to identify oneself with its denial of full humanity for women—has appeal for many of us who have stayed. But we have decided to stay. Why? Because, alongside the androcentric teachings in the tradition, we find meaningful, empowering messages as well. The creation story teaches us to value all persons—indeed, to value the entire created world (the doctrine of creation is a powerful reminder to us to do just that). The Jesus we see in the gospels models a loving, affirming, healing way of relating to people. Further, the Christian tradition teaches us to struggle for justice. This struggle must take place within the church as well as outside it—for the sake of the gospel itself. How can we reconcile the liberating heritage of the good news with the claim that a male Jesus is the Christ? Can this claim about Jesus be affirmed without diminishing the worth of women? How much of the symbol of the redemptive Christ can be maintained—in the interests of the justice and liberation proclaimed by the gospel itself—and how much is unhelpful and detrimental to women?

Before I begin to explore this question I must deal with the objection that we have no right to tamper with received tradition. Such an objection is based on a view of the Bible as a "mythical archetype" which is static, expressing the unchanging will of an unchanging God. A much more helpful understanding of the scriptures and of church tradition is to see it as a "historical root-model" interacting, in a dialectical way, with our own life and experience (Schüssler Fiorenza, 10). This understanding gives us the freedom to utilize the liberating traditions within the Bible in a way which enhances women's struggle for self-affirmation, and to deny authority to the androcentric biblical traditions which are oppressive and destructive (Schüssler Fiorenza, 60).

Claiming this freedom, then, I should like to look at three contemporary feminist theologians who have challenged the male-dominated Christological tradition and have presented us with some very fruitful ways of thinking about Jesus in our twentieth-century context.

Metaphorical Christology

Sallie McFague invites us to a metaphorical understanding of the Christian message, and in particular to a metaphorical understanding of Jesus. Through metaphors we make connections between unlike things; metaphors undercut literalism because a metaphor, as a new and unconventional interpretation of reality, means that the two objects both *are* and *are not* like each other. She asserts that our era has lost the classic view that all of creation is imbued with God's presence, and that the entire natural world is analogous to the divine. Therefore metaphorical theology is more meaningful to our time than analogical theology is. Furthermore, metaphorical theology is internally appropriate to the Christian faith (McFague, 14). Jesus used parables to share his understanding of the realm of God. In this way he modeled a surprising, new way to live.

Metaphorical theology celebrates the parables of Jesus and sees Jesus himself as a parable of God. As opposed to incarnational Christology, which sees Jesus as "the Godhead, veiled in flesh," parabolic Christology is *not* Jesusolatry. A parabolic understanding sees Jesus' life as a story involving surprise, unconventionality, and incongruity. It rejects any idolatry or any identification of a finite creature with God, including Jesus of Nazareth, who both *is* and *is not* God. Yet parabolic theology recognizes that parables do tell us something about the realm of God, and Jesus does show us concretely what God is like (McFague, 18-19). Using Jesus as model we can imagine God primarily in personal images (as mother, father, lover, friend, liberator). McFague insists that these images do not constitute anthropomorphism. Instead, they are necessary to a religious understanding of God. But they are not adequate by themselves; they need to be supplemented by naturalistic images such as God as a rock, a running stream, the sun. She finds many images necessary to avoid idolatry, to express the varied ways of experiencing the divine, and to evoke awe. She suggests that parables are a significant resource to feminists because they do *not* sanctify hierarchical relationships. Instead, they frustrate expectations. As metaphors, they *fit* and *do not fit* the surprising commonwealth of God (McFague, 21).

Rather than the orthodox approach to Christology from above, parabolic Christology begins with the person of Jesus and his work, particularly with the story of Jesus in the synoptics. Since a parabolic approach says Jesus *is* and *is not* God, it relativizes Jesus' particularity at the same time that it universalizes the God whom Jesus metaphorically represents. In this way it makes room for the claims of other religions that they metaphorically express the divine. Denying Jesus' identity with God is important for women who feel excluded by Jesus' maleness (McFague, 51–52).

In addition, seeing Jesus as a parable of God shows us a way of being in the world which is personal, relational, intimate, trusting. Jesus' own relationships with all people, particularly with foreigners, the poor, outcasts, and women, show that a concern for ethics must be at the heart of Christology (McFague, 52). Jesus shows us a God who identifies Godself at whatever cost with the victims of evil. And as Jesus is a parable of God, so are we parables of Jesus. Yet, while we respect his way of being in the world and we reflect Jesus' sense of God in our own lives, we see that his is not the only way; our ways may differ (McFague, 54).

McFague finds significant ramifications for the theory of salvation in her understanding of Jesus' showing us a friendship relationship with God. The orthodox view of salvation has seen God as all-powerful protector and savior, and the atoning work of Jesus as objective, in terms of ransom or substitution; only the Word made flesh can reunite us to God. This approach allows no cooperation on our part. Jesus' model of relationship with God does not support such a one-sided view of salvation. Jesus does not bring about a change in God's attitude toward us but models God as friend. The friendship modeled by Jesus stresses support, mutuality, and solidarity with others and the world. Instead of salvation being totally the work of God, our salvation depends partly on us, our cooperation, our struggle. We cannot avoid our own responsibility by childishly running to a father who will protect and save us. This understanding of salvation does not provide the objective certainty of traditional views, yet objectivity and certainty are elusive in our pluralistic and relative world. This view emphasizes our responsibility together with God's; it sees God as working through us, in total solidarity with us, for salvation (McFague, 185–86).

Sacramental Christology

Carter Heyward also stresses a cooperative relationship between God and humanity. Like McFague she rejects a lofty, all-powerful deity who redeems us by delivering us from the human condition. She points out that God's relationship with Israel as recorded in the Hebrew Bible was one of mutual action, responsiveness, communication, and co-creation (Heyward, 1982:1–3).

Unlike McFague's metaphorical theology, however, which stresses the discontinuity between the human and the divine, Heyward makes no such drastic distinction; her theology is thoroughly sacramental. We experience God in each other rather than experiencing a *wholly other* God (Heyward, 1982:5). An important symbol of the continuity between divine and human is the Christ image. Whether we believe Jesus to be the unique revelation of God to the world or the representation of our capacity to be Christ to the world, we see in Christ the divine and the human in one reality, together (Heyward, 1984:46). Jesus showed us that Christ means a relationship of love between human and divine, manifest in a human life lived in right relationship to God (Heyward, 1984:17–18).

Heyward asks why Christology is an important question and answers that there is no more basic a problem for feminists in the Christian tradition than Jesus. Exclusive focus on this male savior figure has marginalized women. Christology as traditionally formulated is inherently anti-women (Heyward, 1982:196). And as women we need to recognize the female revelations of God who are around us. But Heyward does not reject the model of Jesus. She finds that Jesus is significant for her, for us. As Christians we find in Jesus a person whom we are able to remember communally; and despite some forms of Christian worship and discipleship, the story of Jesus is a compelling motivation to her to struggle for justice for all (Heyward, 1982:197).

Unlike McFague, who substitutes a parabolic Christology for an incarnational understanding, Heyward makes the incarnational affirmation that our bodies are holy (Heyward, 1984:196). Her incarnational Christology, however, differs from orthodox Christology. She faults the tradition for understanding the incarnation as God's coming down to earth. This view wrongly neglects the human role in incarnation, and sees Jesus as a divine person instead of as a human person who loved God. The Nicaean and Chalcedonian creeds mistakenly found significance primarily in who Jesus was—a fully human and fully divine person (Heyward, 1982:32).

Heyward finds the emphasis on what Jesus did—encouraged, healed, valued, befriended, and comforted others—much more helpful. Jesus' actions portrayed the human potential to embody God in the world—a potential which we share (Heyward, 1982:34). Jesus is able to be a real model for us since he is truly human (Heyward, 1982:197).

Jesus' mission—and ours—is to make God incarnate without either confusing ourselves with God or contrasting ourselves with God. What Jesus spoke of as the "kingdom of God" is a commonwealth of divine-human interaction (Heyward, 1982:43–44).

Heyward suggests that instead of thinking of Jesus as "the Son of God," we think of him as our brother. Like McFague, Heyward finds it helpful to reject the understanding of Jesus' death as a ransom paid for our sins. She asserts that in his death his followers realized the importance of his way of life. His death was unnecessary, unjust, and final—a contemptuous rejection of his way of life, which prioritized love of human beings and God. Whatever the resurrection means, it does not negate the injustice of Jesus' crucifixion. Nor does the crucifixion mean that Christians should seek pain. She also criticizes a theology of glory which denies the reality of injustice and suffering (Heyward, 1982:57–58).

She does not reject the possibility of Jesus' physical resurrection but does not see a literal understanding of it as central to Christian faith. The Christian way is, instead, an *ethical* way; like McFague she asserts the primacy of ethics. She envisages the resurrection as an event in the lives of Jesus' friends, who carried on the intimate and immediate relationship with God and other people which Jesus had patterned for them (Heyward, 1982:58–59).

Using the category of friendship, as did McFague, Heyward images Jesus as a messianic friend. Yet Jesus is not the sole messianic friend figure; other people, affirms Heyward, act as messianic friends to us, comforting us, and encouraging us and—since messianic friendship is a reciprocal relationship—being comforted and encouraged by us (Heyward, 1982:165).

Not only is the friendship motif common to McFague and Heyward, the condemnation of Jesusolatry or Christolatry is found in both theologies as well. Heyward rejects Christolatry because it does not take seriously Jesus' mutually messianic presence or our responsibility to be messianic friends to each other. Christolatry prevents us from trying to incarnate God in our own lives (Heyward, 1982:168).

Heyward finds the example of Jesus' life exhilarating. Jesus lived and died to show us what being human is all about. He had the freedom to be himself and therefore we have that freedom as well—and a responsibility to reveal God to each other. Like Jesus, we too are human; like him we are able to re-create the world! (Heyward, 1982:202–3).

Antipatriarchal Christology

Rosemary Radford Ruether shares, in her theology generally and her Christology particularly, this passion "to change the world" (see Ruether, 1981). She presents a historical analysis of Christological development in the Jewish and Christian traditions and then goes on to offer her own understanding of Jesus. First she looks at the ancient roots of Christological thought and finds in pre-Hebraic religions a Goddess who resurrects the vegetation king in annual world renewal (Canaanite and ancient Near Eastern forms of worship) and a divine wisdom figure of the Goddess (East Mediterranean religions). This idea of divine wisdom as a female figure made its way into Hebrew thought—Proverbs 8 and the Wisdom of Solomon (Ruether, 1983:117).

Yet the New Testament used the male symbol of the *Logos* or Son of God to describe what is theologically identical to this *female* figure of divine wisdom. An unfortunate connection is made—and mistakenly deemed to be a necessary ontological link—between the maleness of the historical Jesus and the maleness of the *Logos* who necessarily discloses a male God (Ruether, 1983:117).

Her work shows that the Christological doctrines formed by the early church differ radically from the Jewish messianic hope (Ruether, 1983:116). The Jewish idea of the Messiah developed as a hope for a future king in the Davidic line who would inaugurate the coming reign of God. The Davidic king was to be a conquering warrior (Ruether, 1983:119).

Yet the Christ of Christian doctrine came to be seen as an incarnate divinity, a bestower of immortality, a self-sacrificing savior. These two concepts are so far from each other that it is no surprise that many Jews did not see in Jesus the Messiah figure. But if Jesus is not unambiguously the fulfillment of Jewish messianic prophecy, how can the Christian tradition inherit the Jewish one and claim to fulfill it? (Ruether, 1982:56–57).

Christian claims to legitimacy would be threatened if the historical Jesus were not related to the incarnate deity, the Christ, proclaimed by Christian faith. If, however, the concept of Christ were a reasonable development based on the early followers' experiences of Jesus, then, since Christian Christology was so different from the Jewish messianic hope, how could it claim to fulfill that Jewish messianic expectation? To solve this problem, explains Ruether, Christological doctrines gradually substituted cosmic salvation for the Jewish messianic hope, while retaining the hellenized form (*Christ*) of the word "*Messiah*" (Ruether, 1982:48–49). Early Christian exegesis of Hebrew biblical texts then misunderstood and distorted prophetic criticism, applying the affirmative side of forgiveness and promise to the Christian faith and the negative side of wrath and rejection to the Jews (Ruether, 1982:61).

Ruether is distressed by this Christian wresting of the Jews' own religious history from them. And she finds the Christian claim of a universal cosmic Christ to be not truly universal but instead triumphalist, absolutizing one particularity (Ruether, 1982:67). To avoid this triumphalism Ruether, like Heyward and McFague, is careful to insist on the relativity of the revelation in Christ. As Christians we find that revelation meaningful, but others experience the divine differently and they bear fruit as well (Ruether, 1982:73).

As Christological doctrines were crystalized, not only did Christianity become anti-Judaic and exclusivistic, it also became patriarchal. Ruether traces this development: the disciples, in line with the Jewish messianic expectation, had hoped for a conquering and victorious Messiah and a world-changing event. Thus the crucifixion devastated them. Then the resurrection led them to believe that Jesus was not a failure and that God would intervene soon to bring about a new heaven and a new earth. Ruether, like Heyward, catches the vision of a charismatic group of followers—men and women—preserving the message of Jesus. These disciples prophesied in his name, seeing Jesus as alive in their midst (Ruether, 1983:122–23).

But time elapsed and no new world came about. As the community was institutionalized and the scriptures, particularly the Gospel of Luke, were written, the imminent eschatological expectation, with socio-political dimensions, which characterized Jesus and his earliest followers was replaced by a spiritualized vision of Christ (Ruether, 1982:58) as the center of history, a revelation of God for all time. This Christ ascended into heaven; no longer did he speak through prophetic followers. Now access to this Christ came only through official apostles—that is, males (Ruether, 1983:124).

Next the Christian church became the imperial religion of the Roman empire. The royal symbolism was recaptured from its messianic context; Christ came to be seen in triumphalist, imperial terms. At this point women continued to be accepted as members of the Christian community, but they were clearly unable to represent Christ, who was, after all, "founder and cosmic governor of the existing social hierarchy and . . . male disclosure of a male God whose normative representative can only be male." The male was seen to be the fullest representative of human nature; the female was viewed as defective. Thus the *Logos* had to become incarnate in a male human being (Ruether, 1983: 125–26) and the logical conclusion of this way of thinking was that God is male.

After tracing the patriarchalization of Christological thought, Ruether surveys alternative Christological emphases within the tradition: androgynous Christologies articulated by mystics and spirit Christologies affirmed by prophecy-emphasizing movements such as Montanism, the Joachite groups, and Shakerism. Though these various understandings of Christ were a much-needed corrective to the misogynist Christology dominant in the tradition, they had their problems as well. The androgynous Christologies were themselves androcentric; and the spirit Christologies made a rather complete break with the historical revelation of Jesus. She wonders if women may have to decide that Jesus cannot be redeemer for us; if we may have to "emancipate ourselves" from the male Christ and look for "a new redemptive disclosure of God and of human possibility in female form" (Ruether, 1983:135).

Ruether decides that the way to look for redemptive possibilities for women in the Jesus/Christ image is to view Jesus as the Christ proleptically instead of with finality. Although Jesus announced the messianic hope, he died in the hope (Ruether, 1982:72). She finds that an understanding of Jesus as God's once-and-for-all self-disclosure repudiates Jesus' own spirit. The church's proclamation that Jesus is savior of the world is a drastic change from Jesus' own preaching about the coming realm of God (Ruether, 1983:122).

Like McFague and Heyward, Ruether returns to the Jesus of the synoptic gospels. She shows Jesus' grounding in the prophetic tradition of Israel (Ruether, 1983:135). He was radical and controversial but not outside the Jewish tradition (Ruether, 1982:63). He proclaimed a gospel which liberates and vindicates the marginalized and oppressed groups of society. He preached a social order based on mutuality, *not* on hierarchy and dominance. Women, as the oppressed of the oppressed, were given special attention and care by Jesus. Jesus protested against relationships of social status based on gender, class, ethnicity, and religious position. He spoke as liberator, not because he was male but because he renounced the social order of domination, and himself embodied a new humanity of mutual service and companionship. Therefore Jesus' maleness is not ultimately significant. It symbolizes the "kenosis of patriarchy." Marginalized women and men who respond to Jesus and his message similarly symbolize rejection of the idolatry of patriarchal systems of domination (Ruether, 1983:136–37).

Jesus saw the coming realm of God as a time when the poor and oppressed and marginalized would be freed of bondage—and he saw this as a political reality taking place on earth. Ruether remarks, as did McFague, on the surprising mission of the Messiah and his followers to reverse the social order, identifying with the lowest members of society instead of the highest. Further, the servanthood to which he called his followers was liberation from bondage to any human masters. Jesus made religious revelation accessible in the present and applicable to those who heard him speak (Ruether, 1983:120–21).

But Ruether cautions against encapsulating Christ the redemptive person and Word of God in the historical Jesus. She points out that Christ is not necessarily male; we can encounter Christ in the form of our sister, as early Christian prophets suggested. Christ, as liberated, new humanity, should be understood dynamically. Christ is not merely in the past but in the future, calling us to continual human liberation (Ruether, 1983:38).

We can see from this brief look at McFague, Heyward, and Ruether the wealth of empowering and liberating images in Jesus' life. It is significant to note that of all the New Testament pictures of Jesus and descriptions of Christ, all three of these feminist theologians are most closely drawn to the Jesus of the synoptic gospels—the Jesus who told parables, who related warmly to other human beings. This is the Jesus with whom all of us—men *and women* of faith—have the most in common. The claims of other traditions within the New Testament and in later centuries of the Christian era—claims about Jesus' death as an atonement for our sins, about the cosmic Christ—are more problematic from a feminist point of view. More work remains to be done in critically exploring these claims to see what can be retained without devaluing women as inferior human beings. But as a twentieth-century feminist I am glad to celebrate Jesus' teachings and ministry and life at the same time that I affirm myself as a woman.

References

Cone, James. 1975. *God of the Oppressed*. New York: Seabury.

Daly, Mary. 1974. *Beyond God the Father: Toward a Philosophy of Women's Liberation*. Boston: Beacon.

Heyward, Irene Carter. 1982. *The Redemption of God: A Theology of Mutual Relation*. Lanham, MD: University Press of America.

———. 1984. *Our Passion for Justice: Images of Power, Sexuality, and Liberation*. New York: Pilgrim.

McFague, Sallie. 1982. *Metaphorical Theology: Models of God in Religious Language*. Philadelphia: Fortress.

Ruether, Rosemary Radford. 1981. *To Change the World: Christology and Cultural Criticism*. New York: Crossroad.

———. 1982. *Disputed Questions: On Being a Christian*. Nashville: Abingdon.

———. 1983. *Sexism and God-Talk: Toward a Feminist Theology*. Boston: Beacon.

Schüssler Fiorenza, Elizabeth. 1984. *Bread not Stone: The Challenge of Feminist Biblical Interpretation*. Boston: Beacon.

PART FOUR

IN THE THIRD WORLD

CHAPTER 7

Contextualizing the Faith: Protestant Churches in Cuba

Paul Deats and Alice Hageman

We assume that some kind of contextualization of the faith (any faith) always occurs. The questions we ought to ask are the following: Is the contextualizing done with critical self-awareness? In terms of what context is the process perceived and carried forward? The latter question implies that there are usually competing contexts, or at the least competing perceptions of any given context.

Changing contexts of Cuban Protestant churches since 1868 include:

1. Ecclesiastical domination by Spanish Roman Catholicism;
2. Cuban nationalism and independence movements beginning in the mid-nineteenth century;
3. An enduring African cultural heritage;
4. United States Protestant mission boards—usually "home" mission boards, typically from churches in the southern United States, and mostly reflective of a denominationally focused enterprise—which entered Cuba with the United States government and United States corporations after 1899;
5. The succession of governments in Cuba—Spanish, United States dominated neocolonial, and revolutionary—with their respective ideologies and practices;
6. Occasional but increasing ecumenical influences, from the World Council of Churches (especially after 1959), from Roman Catholicism reflecting Vatican II and the 1968 Medellín Conference, and from other Latin American experiences.

Before the Revolution

Almost every careful observer of Cuba prior to the Revolution of 1959 has noted that Cuba differed from almost all the rest of Latin American cultures in that it was for a long time a "secular" culture, with no deep penetration into the life of the people by any faith except for *santeria*, a syncretic blending of Yoruba religion brought from West Africa with a panoply of Catholic saints. Of the 1959 population, about 75 percent were nominal Catholics; Protestants counted less than 5 percent.

Because the authors are more familiar with the life of the Protestant churches, this essay will primarily consider that segment of Cuban religious life.

1868–1898: Patriotic Protestantism

Despite its lack of penetration into popular piety, Spanish Roman Catholicism had been in Cuba since 1494. The first Protestant worship service was held aboard a United States gunboat anchored in the Port of Havana in 1871, presided over by an American Episcopal bishop (see Adolfo Ham Reyes, 332). In 1871 Edward Kenney came to Cuba as an Episcopal missionary to visiting seamen.

It is important to note that Cuban tobacco workers and *independentistas* had fled to Florida during the 1850s and 1860s. There some became converts to Protestantism. Many also had contact with José Martí, the father figure of the Cuban Revolution, who was also in exile in the United States. One Cuban pastor, Rafael Cepeda, has posited that, although Martí continued to point out shortcomings in Protestantism, he also supported it "for being anticlerical and antidogmatic, and praised some Protestant leaders for their social principles of loyalty to the people, the common people."

These exiles returned to Cuba following 1868 to try to free Cuba from Spanish oppression and ecclesiastical domination. Their Protestantism became identified with Cuban independence. Their influence spread among tobacco workers, trading house clerks, African slaves, Chinese coolies, the lower middle class and the poor. The few missionaries from the United States who went to Cuba in this period were "guests." The context of the Protestantism of these returned exiles was an avowedly Cuban patriotism.

1898–1940: Neocolonial Shift in Context

With the end of Spanish rule over Cuba, and the new period of so-called independence (that is, independence from Spain, but increasing dependency on the United States), the patriotism of Cuban Protestantism shifted from Cuba to the United States. For mission boards in the United States, Cuba and the Philippines became the new targets.

Theo Tschuy (see Tschuy, 1978) records that at this time Protestant denominations from the mainland swept aside the Cuban patriotic leaders of the earlier period and sought, successfully, to extend their denominational system unchanged to the soil and culture of the newly independent island. The revolutionary church of the late nineteenth century became submerged and largely invisible, only to resurface at critical moments, especially in the 1950s.

The mission churches were dependent on the sending bodies for funds, personnel, and basic theological and liturgical orientation; the context was the relatively individualistic and conservative denominationalism of the southern United States. J. Merle Davis concludes:

> Thus it came about that the Church which arose in Cuba is a Church that is too costly to be carried by the economic power of its membership, and calls for an organization, program, ritual, and discipline which is some- what foreign to the inheritance of the Cuban People [Davis, 78].

Davis goes on to note, under "Obstacles to Church Growth," the economic disparities made evident by tourists who visited from the United States (half a million in 1940). Many observers saw the Variel exodus four decades later, in 1980, as at least in large part due to the impression made by exiles returning to Cuba with gifts for their families—that the United States was a paradise with streets paved with gold. Davis, who had made similar studies in Mexico and other poorer countries, continued with this observation:

> The American type of Church is not adjusted to the Cuban economy because it is essentially a middle-class institution with strong middle-class support. A middle-class institution has been set up in Cuba in an eco- nomic and social order in which the middle-class, as known in America, practically does not exist. The inevitable has happened. The Cuban church has been supported in the main by the gifts of the middle-class Christians of the United States.
>
> *We have here reached the crux of the economic problem of the mission- ary church—not only in Cuba but in many other lands. How can a relatively expensive institution, a product of an alien, high grade econ- omy and living standards, be indigenized and financed in countries of lower economic standards where the bulk of the church members are drawn from the classes of the lower economic levels?* [Davis, 79–80, emphasis added].

Only the Baptists of the eastern part of Cuba, who were cut off from United States funding, showed signs of autonomy, but even they were not yet, when Davis wrote in 1942, mature in independence. Later observers note that there was less of an exodus from that region in the early years following the Revolution.

One other group which seems to stand outside the historic churches deserves mention—Los Pinos Nuevos. This group was formed in the second decade of this century, by Presbyterian missionaries. Its origins are said to be Cuban in principles, government, and financial support, thus more "pure." However, its *Las Doctrinas Fundamentales de la Fe Cristiana*, from about 1936, was edited in English, by a North American, and translated into Spanish in the United

States before being sent to Cuba! This seems to indicate theological dependence comparable to the missionary churches established earlier; it is not the fruit of a contextualized reflection by Cubans (or even by missionaries serving in Cuba).

Israel Batista, biblical scholar and librarian, comments that the economic influence of the model imported from the United States was so intrinsic that it was a factor of which Cuban Christians themselves were hardly aware. And this despite the avowal by the best mission leaders that they sought to implant the "pure gospel!" Few were able to transcend identification of that gospel with the American way of life (see Reyes, 334–35).

Let us suggest, drawing on Batista and Tschuy principally, six characteristics of this period:

1. Dependency, as noted above, which was both economic and cultural.

2. Influence of home mission boards of southern denominations—theologically conservative, suspicious of the "modernism" of the emerging ecumenical movement (actually protecting Cubans from the debates over scripture in the denominations themselves), racist in practice and too often in theory; and liturgically reflecting revival individualism.

3. Anti-Catholic—defensive against the Roman Catholic Church, but at once triumphalistic in relation to Protestant ecumenism.

4. Divided—what Batista labels a reductive ecumenism. Comity agreements meant that southern and northern Baptist mission boards divided Cuba into east and west, respectively. In the 1920s fundamentalist sects asserted their competitiveness over against even the reductive ecumenism of comity agreements. (Here there should be added a note on Seventh Day Adventists, who reflected not the south but the north and west of the United States. Their work was highly dependent on distribution of tracts, at a time when half the population was unable to read! They began their work in rural areas, on sites provided by North American corporations. Pay differentials between North Americans and Cuban nationals were comparable to those of other bodies, and North Americans retained most leadership positions. Caleb Rosado has written a dissertation focused on the Adventists: "Sect and Party: Religion under Revolution in Cuba" (Northwestern University, 1985).

5. An urban church, with the main vehicle of evangelization being private schools.

6. A "pure" church, professedly resistant to syncretism in its new environment. Adolfo Ham Reyes quotes Methodist Bishop W. A. Candler in 1909: "We did not come with any political mission"; and despite ministers' concern for the political well-being of the island "which they love so much, they have not meddled in political matters or taken part in partisan questions" (Reyes, 327). In the following article, Carlos M. Camps Cruell writes: "Missionary efforts have always been defined as apolitical. They openly approved the legitimacy of the new economic, social and political order that emerged in 1899, however" (Cruell, 340).

It was against this background that certain changes began to occur, in

Christians in access to some areas of higher education and some types of work, remained matters of serious concern.

The late 1960s ended relatively quietly, and were marked by a move toward what might be termed "peaceful co-existence." By 1969 the Cuban Catholic bishops, in a pastoral letter to the faithful of the island nation, called for an end to the United States embargo. The first groups of priests and pastors participating in the volunteer work of assisting in the nation's sugar harvest were organized.

1969-1980: Period of Peaceful Coexistence

For the Cuban government, just as the early years of the Revolution were a time for consolidating its power in the face of increasing opposition both inside and outside Cuba, so the 1970s represented a period of institutionalization of socialist patterns. In 1975 the first congress of the Cuban Communist Party (Partido Comunista de Cuba—hereafter, PCC) was held. During this same period a new constitution was adopted, as well as a family code which attempted to set forth socialist norms for relations between men and women, and for children within families. The system of *Poder Popular*, "popular power," local elections of officials who would coordinate and oversee the daily work-ings of municipalities, was also instituted.

During this period, Fidel Castro, who has been and remains the chief articulator of the goals and positions of the Cuban Revolution, made two major statements outside Cuba regarding the role of religion in the Revolution. In December 1971, during an official state visit to the Allende government in Chile, and again in October 1977, during a meeting in Jamaica with leaders of the World Council of Churches, Fidel spoke about the possibility of a "strate-gic alliance" between Christians and Marxists. At the latter gathering he affirmed that, "it isn't enough to respect each other, we must cooperate with each other in order to change the world." He went on to assert that "there are no contradictions between religion and socialism."

In the churches, the overt hostility of the 1960s had subsided; a mood of resignation, and attempts to make the best of a situation characterized in mostly negative though occasionally positive terms, were substituted. Some moves were made toward some sort of rapprochement, a more positive viewing of the circumstances in which Cuban Christians now found themselves. One official church statement indicative of this movement is the statement of faith of the Presbyterian-Reformed Church of Cuba, formulated in 1977. This statement emphasizes that the human being is a steward of God-given re-sources. It attempts to give a more positive and hopeful interpretation of the opportunities for Christians inherent in life in a socialist society.

1980-1988: Period of Rapprochement

Since 1980 major strides have been made in relations between church and state in Cuba, and thus in the context in which Cuban Christians practice their the United States, lay leadership emerged in central positions.

Once economic ties with the United States had been severed for churches as well as the society as a whole, new sources of economic support had to be developed, both within congregations and internationally. The Cuba Project, administered by the World Council of Churches in Geneva, was one means by which mission boards in the United States provided some continued assistance and maintained some continuing contact with Protestant communities in Cuba. The Cuba Project also broadened to European churches, West and East, the base of external economic as well as theological support for Cuban Protestants.

The early 1960s saw major confrontations between the Cuban Roman Catholic Church and the government. Some Catholic leaders spoke vigorously against the atheist ideology of the government. Prime Minister Fidel Castro charged religious leaders with being hypocrites, "whitewashed tombs," failing to practice during the repressive Batista era what they preached now as requirements for the new government. The rhetoric and activity of the early 1960s pitted supporters of the "religious" position against supporters of the government. These confrontations had repercussions on the Protestant community, creating a climate of mutual distrust between "believer" and "revolutionary."

The conflict came to a head in September 1961 with a Catholic religious procession which led to fighting in the streets and resulted in the expulsion of Catholic religious workers who were foreign nationals, primarily from Franco's Spain. An exchange of invective ensued, although Fidel Castro continued to make careful distinctions between the teachings of Jesus Christ, and past and present practices of the churches, especially the dominant Catholic Church.

A low point in relations between church and state was reached when, in the period between November 1965 and June 1968, a number of priests and ministers were placed in agricultural labor "reeducation" camps, in an effort to deal with the problem perceived by the government of counter-revolutionary attitudes and antisocial activity on the part of the clergy. Internments lasted from a few months to more than two years.

As the overt hostilities between churches and government subsequently subsided, the churches settled for maintaining the worship and educational life of their congregations. Street processions, the setting for some of the earlier direct confrontations, were prohibited, as was street-corner evangelization. With nationalization in 1961 of church-related schools and most church-sponsored hospitals, a major raison d'être for the churches was eliminated. The churches, Catholic and Protestant alike, were looked upon, both within and without, as a place of refuge, and participation in church life was for many a sign of passive disaffection with the Revolution. Worship was oriented toward the comfort of individuals; its nostalgic characteristics harkened to what was perceived to be a better and more propitious past. The teaching of Marxism-Leninism in the public schools, and discrimination against avowed were now disadvantaged in favor of the countryside. Economic, social, cultural and ideological patterns and priorities changed. Both Protestant and Catholic churches, and their faithful, had great difficulty changing with them.

In response to the question frequently put to him in Western countries, "How is it possible to be a Christian in a communist country?," Sergio Arce, professor of theology at the Protestant seminary in Matanzas, and for fifteen years its rector, has responded, "How is it possible to be a Christian in a capitalist country?" Those two questions, and their responses, have over-shadowed much of the life of churches in Cuba since the early years of the Cuban Revolution.

1959-1969: Church-State Mutual Distrust

Considering the question, "Were the churches prepared for the Revolution?,"[1] most observers agree that the response is an emphatic "NO!" Although there were a few notable exceptions (including martyred revolutionary heroes such as Frank and Josué Pais, sons of a Baptist pastor from Santiago de Cuba, and José Antonio Echevarría, a Catholic student who led the March 1957 assault on the presidential palace in Havana), most self-identified Christians took no active role in the struggles against the dictator Batista during the insurrectionary period, 1953-1958. In 1959 and the early 1960s, when the Revolution had moved in a socialistic direction beyond "liberal" expectations, dependence on the United States bore its bitter fruit. Many religious leaders—Catholic, Protestant, and Jewish—left the country. Those fleeing included most of the Methodist pastors, half of the Methodist lay leaders, as well as half of all Presbyterian ministers and Episcopal priests. All Protestant missionaries also left, except for a Presbyterian music teacher, Lois Kroehler. She stayed on because of her solidarity with the Cuban people. Her commitment to service, identifying with the Christian community and with the main goals of the Revolution, led to her being respected and loved by Protestants in particular, and Cubans generally.

With the identification of Cuban political and economic life with social-ism, and with the break in diplomatic relations with the United States, many churches went into virtual exile. The exodus of many church-related persons, leaders and lay alike, seems to bear some direct relation to the extent to which their churches were economically and structurally dependent on United States churches. Those who left, especially those who had been deeply engaged in the life of the churches, were persuaded that they would no longer be able to be practicing Christians in a revolutionary (by April 1961 explicitly socialist) society. By and large those who stayed shared those apprehensions, but for one reason or another decided to remain and share the fate of their nation, although many adopted the modus vivendi of an internal exile. The exodus produced some unforeseen results; for example, in the Methodist Church, which saw most of its clergy leave for advance of the changes which would be called for following the Revolution in 1959.

1940-1959: Emerging Ecumenism and Social Awareness

In 1942 the Cuban Council of Evangelical Churches was born, following a visit by the world leader, John R. Mott. Council activities reflected little emphasis on faith and order or on church and society—critical ecumenical areas of work; the focus was on mission and evangelism. Still, observers noted, there was now a forum for encounter among the previously divided bodies, as well as an instrument with which the government could be confronted. (The secretary of the new council was a missionary, S. A. Neblett, who had torpedoed the first effort to form such a group in 1916, a quarter of a century earlier.)

In 1946 Methodists, Presbyterians, and Episcopalians united their theological training efforts in the Evangelical Seminary at Matanzas, still the only truly ecumenical seminary in Cuba.

Also in 1946 came the founding of the (largely Methodist) Movimiento Social Cristiano, which sought to find a way between capitalism and communism. Later this movement became the social action department of the Cuban Council of Evangelical Churches (about 1949).

Some Protestant leaders supported the Cuban underground against the dictator Batista, in order to "clean out" Cuba of the gambling, prostitution, and alcohol perceived to be linked with the Batista government's promotion of tourism. Tschuy interprets their expectations as a liberal revolution, getting rid of the dictator, then returning to business as usual (in a neocolonial, dependent situation).

Since the Revolution

The year 1959 represents for Cuban society a sharp break with all that had formerly characterized it. Ties were severed with the United States, geographically its nearest neighbor and economically its twentieth-century primary support (through purchase of the bulk of the annual production of Cuban sugar). By 1961 the United States had become Cuba's principal adversary. The apparently unresolvable conflicts between the United States and Cuba culminated in 1961 with the break in diplomatic relations, a situation which has since been only slightly ameliorated with the establishment, in 1977, of "Interest Sections" lodged in the respective former embassies of both countries. Cuba developed new relationships with the Soviet Union and other countries in Eastern Europe. An inclusive economic embargo imposed by the United States after the break in diplomatic relations totally altered previous consumer and industrial patterns: spare parts for machinery were no longer available, nor were familiar United States imports any longer available in the stores. With the emphasis placed on development in rural areas—in an attempt to provide education, medical care, and housing for all—the previously privileged cities faith. Many influences have led to this change on the part of both church and state, including the meeting of the Latin American Catholic bishops in Medellín in 1968, the growing influence of the perspective of liberation theology in both theoretical constructs and the daily practice of Christians throughout Latin America, and the role of Christians in the new era instituted with the Sandinista triumph in Nicaragua in 1979.

This change was reflected in a speech given by Fidel Castro to the Cuban people on July 26, 1980, one week after his visit to Nicaragua on the occasion of the first anniversary of the new Nicaragua. Reflecting on the challenge of a Maryknoll sister to reformulate his thinking about the relations of Christians and Marxists, Fidel said:

> And some religious leaders in Nicaragua asked us why strategic alliance . . . why not speak of unity between Marxist-Leninists and Christians? I don't know what the imperialists think about this. But I'm absolutely convinced the formula is highly explosive. It exists not only in Nicaragua but also in El Salvador, where the revolutionary forces and Christian forces are closely united [Castro, July 27, 1980].

A further reflection of the change of formulation, as well as of practice, came when Jesse Jackson, then a candidate for nomination as the Democratic Party's presidential candidate, visited Cuba in June 1984. Toward the end of his visit he invited Fidel to accompany him to a Protestant church service. Fidel accepted the invitation, and for the first time since leaving the Sierra Maestra in early 1959 attended a service of Christian worship.

In January 1985 a delegation from the United States Conference of Catholic Bishops visited their Cuban counterparts, and during the course of their stay had a lengthy interview with Fidel Castro. The following month, an official Department of Religious Affairs of the PCC was established, headed by Dr. José Felipe Carneado. Although Dr. Carneado had for some time been charged with primary responsibility for governmental relations with churches in Cuba, he had previously done so in addition to a number of other responsibilities. Since the establishment of the Department of Religious Affairs, ecclesiastical concerns constitute Dr. Carneado's total portfolio.

Perhaps the culmination of this process of mutual rapprochement took place in December 1985, with the publication of *Fidel y la Religión* (*Fidel and Religion*). This is a transcription of a series of interviews with Fidel conducted in the spring of 1985 by the Brazilian Dominican, Frei Betto. The first printing of this book was sold out within a few days of its appearance in Cuba; by the fall of 1986 some one million copies published in Cuba were in circulation. Reports indicate that the subject of religion in general, and liberation theology in particular, have been a significant topic for general Cuban conversation since the book's publication. In this book, Fidel discusses a variety of issues: the early influence of the Jesuits who provided his education; his basic view (frequently reiterated since he came to prominence in the 1960s) of the words and work of Jesus Christ; the role of liberation theology in struggles for liberation throughout Latin America; the potential for collaboration between Christians and Marxists in attaining shared goals.

Shifts in perspective and practice have not been only on the part of the Cuban government. In February 1986 the Roman Catholic Church of Cuba held the "National Ecclesial Encounter" in Havana, a week-long gathering of delegates from the various dioceses in the country. This gathering was the culmination of a seven-year process of study and reflection in each diocese on the life of the church in contemporary Cuba.

A published working document developed through the preparation process provided the basis for the discussions at the encounter (see *Documento,* Mayo, 1986). This document accepted the following as the homework of the encounter: to reconsider the Roman Catholic past in Cuba; to recognize errors; to transform pastoral structures for more effective service to social life; and to renew the faith. The teachings of Pope John Paul II provided the basis for the three goals proposed in the document for the synthesis of culture and faith:

1. To put the dynamics of Christian love at the service of society as an element of reconciliation, dialogue, and unity;
2. To enrich in the emerging lifestyle those values which the gospel can contribute;
3. To indicate and aid in remedying obstacles to prevent human dignity and essential national identity.

There are fundamental differences between the Christian faith and the Marxist ideology, the document notes, but these do not stand in the way of constructive dialogue and collaboration. One sign that relations between church and state were more flexible in 1986 than in 1961 is the fact that lay delegates were given leave from their work places to attend this week-long meeting. It is notable that those assembled on the platform for that gathering included the Archbishop of Havana, Jaime Ortega; the Papal Nuncio in Cuba, Giulio Einaudi; special papal envoy Cardinal Eduardo Pironio (president of the Pontifical Council of the Laity); José Felipe Carnedo, head of the PCC Department of Religious Affairs; and Deputy Foreign Minister of the Republic of Cuba, Ricardo Alarcón. Such an event, gathered to consider the mission of the church in Cuba, attended by representatives from Rome and from the Cuban government, would have been unimaginable until quite recently! With this encounter, as symbolized by both its preparatory document and the spirit of its participants, Cuban Roman Catholics seem to be moving to overcome their relative isolation from the Revolution in its early years.

The "New Sects"

We have dealt mainly with the mainline Protestant denominations. We turn now to a brief comment on the sects, drawing largely on Pablo Richard's "Central America: Sects Use Marketing Techniques, Dollars to 'Sell' Gospel" and the Roman Catholic Bishops' of Central America pastoral letter, "Our Salvation Is Christ." Both the Catholic bishops and such leaders as Fidel

Castro are concerned about the "new sects," apparently with finance and direction from the United States. These sects stand in opposition to the popular Christian movements in Central America, and to the Revolution in Cuba and Nicaragua. Richard thinks they have a clear anti-communist orientation, and that some cooperate with counter-insurgency groups opposing popular governments (Richard, 5).

The "new sects" have not themselves come into Cuba; however, there are groups there with similar tendencies, which were there before the Revolution, and which are seen by the Cuban Communist Party and government as "counterrevolutionary" (see *Tesis y Resoluciones*, 315–17). The Jehovah's Witnesses are the sect that causes most concern in Cuba.

Concluding Comments

This review began with the assumption that contextualization of the faith— of some kind—always occurs. What have we learned about more than a century of the Cuban experience, so briefly covered here?

Our first question asked whether the contextualizing was done with critical self-awareness. The first three decades (1868–1898) of the prerevolutionary period among Protestants seem to have been characterized by the most critical self-awareness, as Cuban exiles became Protestant converts and returned to lead what Tschuy calls "patriotic Protestantism." Cubans writing later testify to a lack of that self-critical adaptation in the first four decades of this century, a taken-for-grantedness about cultural and financial dependence on the United States. In the two decades prior to the Revolution, there were new stirrings of a more critical spirit and sporadic signs of the reemergence of the submerged revolutionary church.

Our second question asked about the specific context involved. The context in the first period of the prerevolutionary period was Cuban nationalism and independence. In the second period the context shifted to the culture and religion of the southern United States. The third period brought an awareness of a more ecumenical context and a new perception of the need for social change in Cuba.

With the 1959 Revolution the context shifted drastically and Protestant churches were forced to become more critically self-aware. No church was prepared for the experience of the Revolution, and many pastors and priests went into foreign exile, congregations and leaders remaining in Cuba often went into internal exile. Total financial dependence on United States churches was ended, and the door was opened to more ecumenical influences though the World Council of Churches.

The early 1960s were a period of confrontation, with churches turning inward to worship and education, the church often serving as refuge from discrimination in education and employment. From 1969 to 1980 more peaceful coexistence came about, with the consolidation of the Revolution, the maturing of new leadership in the churches, and the increasing significance of liberation theology for all Latin American Christians. Since 1980 there has developed a more positive rapprochement between the churches and the government.

Cuban colleagues have raised with the authors of this essay the question of what we think the churches in Cuba and their sponsors in the United States might have done, or should have done, differently. We do not feel qualified to make such a judgment, after the fact, in abstraction, but we do venture the modest hope that some churches might learn from some implications we draw from this specific study of contextualization:

1. Whatever the context—whether in a situation of relative security and religious liberty, or in a more threatening and overtly restrictive situation; whether as a dependent "receiving" church, or a dominant "sending" church, or a church engaged in mutual interchange—it is important to exercise critical self-awareness of competing contexts, paying particular attention to the immediate context of a particular church, so that any choices made will be conscious and more responsible, and judgments can be nuanced.

2. Churches in presumed secure and "safe" contexts should exercise considerable restraint of judgment and an appropriate humility when assessing the responses of other churches caught in contexts of rapid change, even revolution.

3. Sometimes churches are isolated from or unconscious of their own immediate contexts—insulated from their socio-economic reality, uninvolved in vigorous theological reflection. If they are subsequently caught up in rapid social change, they may experience "cultural schizophrenia," conflict between their dependency on what has been and that source of support, and their loyalties to what might be best for the whole of their nation. "Sending churches," such as those in the United States and Western Europe, could seek to understand more clearly the impact of their presence—and that of other representatives from their country—on other contexts in which churches find themselves.

4. Continuing and genuine engagement in the ecumenical movement (for Roman Catholics, conciliar enterprises growing out of Vatican II such as CELAM; for Protestants, activities engendered by the World Council of Churches) may help sharpen self-critical awareness, facilitate freer communication across barriers, and provide mutual support.

Note

1. Protestant churches provide the main reference for these comments; however, much of the dynamic described characterizes Catholic churches as well. Although most examples are drawn from Protestant sources, some specific examples come from the experience of Catholic churches.

References

Arce, Sergio. 1985. *The Church and Socialism: Reflections from a Cuban Context.* New York: Circus.

Castro, Fidel. Speech. Reprinted in *Granma*, July 27, 1980.

Cruell, Carlos M. Camps. July 1985. "Social Implications of the Missionary Heritage," in *International Review of Missions*, 337–42.

Davis, J. Merle. 1942. *The Cuban Church in a Sugar Economy*. International Missionary Council.

Documento. Mayo 1986. Mexico City: Centro Regional de Informaciones Ecuménicas, A.C., año IX, n. 41.

Fernandez, Manuel. *Religíon y Revolucíon en Cuba*. ILACDE (Box 39, Jackson Heights, Flushing, NY 11372).

Fidel y la Religíon: Conversaciones con Frei Betto. 1985. Havana: Oficina de Publicaciones del Consejo de Estado. Available in Spanish from the Center for Church Studies, 124 West 23rd St., New York, NY 10114. English translation, Simon and Schuster, 1987.

Hageman, Alice, and Paul Deats. 1985. "Cuba," in *Three Worlds of Christian-Marxist Encounters*. Nicholas Piediscalzi and Robert G. Thobaben, eds. Philadelphia: Fortress, pp. 173–92.

Hageman, Alice, and Philip Wheaton. 1971. *Religion in Cuba Today: New Church in a New Society*. Association Press.

Ramos, Marcos Antonio. 1986. *Panorama del Protestantismo en Cuba*. Miami: Editorial Caribe.

Reyes, Adolfo Han. July 1985. "An Ecumenical Perspective on the Cuban Protestant Missionary Heritage," in *International Review of Missions*, 327–36.

Richard, Pablo. May 9, 1985. "Central America: Sects Use Marketing Techniques, Dollars to 'Sell' Gospel," in *Latin America Press,* vol. 17, 5–8, Lima.

Roman Catholic Bishops of Central America. September 1981. "Our Salvation Is in Christ" (pastoral letter).

Tesis y Resoluciones. 1978. Primer congreso del Partido Comunista de Cuba 1975. Havana: Editorial de Ciencias Sociales, 295–323.

Tschuy, Theo. 1978. *Hundert Jahre Kabanischer Protestantismus (1868–1961),* Frankfurt: Peter Lang Verlag.

CHAPTER 8

Basic Ecclesial Communities: A New Model of Church

Jeanne Gallo

In the Foreword to Alvaro Barreiro's *Basic Ecclesial Communities: The Evangelization of the Poor,* a North American minister, Allan Deck, writes:

> There are real indications that the dramatic renewal of the Church in Latin America is making itself felt in the universal Church and specifically in the North American Catholic Community. Three realities—all rooted in the socio-economic, political, and cultural complexities of Latin America—are powerfully contributing to an awakening of consciences and a deepening of awareness: the Latin American theology of liberation, the gruesome struggle for liberation now taking place especially in Central America, and the refreshing emergence of the Basic Ecclesial Communities [Barreiro, x].

These three realities—liberation theology, liberation struggles, and the emergence of basic ecclesial communities (*comunidades de base*)—are giving shape to a new church. The CEBs, the grassroots nuclei of this emerging "church of the poor," constitute its cornerstone; at the same time, they are fast becoming a major political force in society at large.

Although liberation theology and liberation struggles are linked to the CEBs, this paper will address specifically CEBs. The other two factors will be touched on as they are directly related to the CEBs.

What Are Basic Ecclesial Communities?

In doing research on the CEBs, there appeared to be any number of ways to define the term. For example:

The CEB is a faith community that gathers somehow/somewhere in prayer and that is also a collective force towards social change [English, January, 1985].

[CEBs] are made up of small groups of an average of ten people; it is most usually a number of these groups—generally ten—grouped in one area, usually a parish, that is known as a [CEB] [C. Boff, 53].

[CEBs] consist of a dozen or few dozen members each and emphasize the active participation of each person in prayer, worship, reflection and action, while creating strong community bonds through this relationship of dialogue and sharing [Hennelly, 62].

A CEB is the Church at its smallest level [Marins, 2].

A CEB is a grouping of a dozen to fifty or more persons, accompanied occasionally by a priest or pastoral agent, who meet to pray and reflect on their everyday lives in the light of the Bible and to celebrate their faith [Kirby and Molineaux, 1].

Basic Christian communities are like living cells in an organism newly coming to life. Generally, twelve to twenty persons make up a community. They usually come together in their neighborhood or village once a week. They read sacred scripture, pray together, and sing hymns. They reflect on what the scriptures mean in their daily lives. That reflection frequently leads them to courses of political action to improve the living conditions in their barrio [Cleary, 104–5].

[CEBs] are places of communion, where the presence of the Kingdom of God, which is a kingdom of justice, peace, and love, is manifested sacramentally, that is, visibly and effectively. They are communities of poor people who are living, and trying to live increasingly, faith, hope, and love [Comblin, 457].

Basic ecclesial communities are agents of evangelization and primordial factor[s] of human promotion and development [Zenteno, 15].

As can be seen from the above definitions, there is no one definition of basic ecclesial communities. Some use the term to describe a small church and some to describe a group of these groups. What the definitions do point out is that the CEBs are not an accomplished fact, but rather they are in an ongoing process of becoming.

Keeping this in mind, in order to get at a more precise meaning of CEB for the purpose of this paper, I will analyze the various meanings that are included in the term "basic ecclesial community." I will use the analysis of José Marins and Frei Betto (both of Brazil). These two have been in contact with the development of CEBs throughout Latin America for many years and have written extensively on them.

As regards the word "basic" Marins distinguishes four levels of meaning:

1. In the *sociological* sense, "basic" means popular, grassroots, closely linked to the people. In Latin America, it refers to those who are at the bottom of society: those who are poor and marginalized in their lives and in their power of decision-making.
2. In the *theological* sense, "basic" refers to the level at which the church functions as a salvific event for real and specific people identifiable here and now. Such a community is basic because it contains all the essential elements of the church as the people of God.
3. In the *descriptive* sense, "basic" refers to the point of origin. It signifies "the vital network of the Church, at the point where it becomes actively present in the world as leaven, salt, light, and as a basic cell of the larger society" (Marins, 18).
4. In the *strategic* or *pastoral* sense, "basic" refers to the institutional need to create a network of communication with the grassroots in order to be "constantly in touch with ever-changing life processes and to direct effective change" (Marins, 18).

The word "ecclesial" signifies that the CEBs' motivational force is "faith in Jesus Christ, the desire to live his commandment of love, to carry out his mission by the power of the Holy Spirit in communion with the local and universal Church" (Marins, 18).

Marins includes a number of distinctions for the meaning of "community." These include a stress on primary relationships, solidarity, mutual help, and a deeper, more stable, joyous communal life. The term also stresses a conscious personal commitment to a common mission along with growth in co-responsibility for the group while experiencing the affirmation of one's own individual identity. It also implies insertion of the community into its own historical reality with all its problems and challenges. It attempts to transform the situation in the light of the Christian vision. With regard to organization, it suggests minimum structures and coordination and maximal emphasis on the life of the community, while respecting the different talents and ministries of each person. Finally, community means that a CEB has its own identity, distinct from other groups and other forms of social structures such as state, society, nation.

At Puebla (1979), the question was asked, "When is a popular group truly a basic ecclesial community?" In a popularized version of the final document, the answer is given:

* As community, when it integrates families, adults, and youth in a friend-ship rooted in the faith.
* As ecclesial, when it is a community of faith, hope and love. When it

celebrates the Word of God and is nourished by the Eucharist—the greatest of sacraments. When it lives the Word of God in solidarity with others, continuing the mission of the Church and joined to the bishop.
* As basic, when it is composed of a small number of poor people, like a permanent cell in the larger community [Betto, 73].

What Do Basic Ecclesial Communities Do?

Because the CEBs are grassroots innovations, they tend to vary from place to place. But there is enough similarity to describe them in common terms.

Lay leaders are the key to the continuity and the dynamism of the CEBs. They assemble the community at least once a week, in a set place, usually a family home, in a chapel, or simply in the shade of a tree.

The community prays, listens to the Word of God, and discusses problems affecting its life. The leader moves the group along. As various actions emerge from the reflection, other persons are called forth to perform certain tasks, depending upon the need of the moment.

The CEBs are communities whose purpose includes action. That action will vary depending upon the level of commitment of the members to their local community and to the society at large. The action may be in the religious domain: catechesis, Bible study, planning a prayer week. It may also be in the social arena: improvements in the neighborhood, collective works, teaching the illiterate to read, doing political and legal education, creating and strengthening trade unions, participation in political activities.

The type and degree of commitment in these areas will depend on the social character of the CEB and the degree of development it has reached. In describing the developmental process of CEBs as he sees it, Leonardo Boff writes:

> This generally began with the reading of the Bible and proceeded to the creation of small base or basic ecclesial communities. Initially, such a community serves to deepen the faith of its members, to prepare the liturgy, the sacraments, and the life of prayer. At a more advanced stage these members begin to help each other. As they become better organized and reflect more deeply, they come to the realization that the problems they encounter have a structural character. . . . Thus, the question of politics arises and the desire for liberation is set in a concrete and historical context [L. Boff, 8].

Whatever action the CEB undertakes, whether religious or social, it comes from the reality of the community and its needs as perceived through the dynamic of analysis, reflection, and dialogue. What is unique about the CEBs is that what is done is done from the perspective of the poor, for by and large these are the people who make up the CEBs.

Here are some examples of what members of CEBs have been led to do:

An old mine worker put in the hands of the youngest miner his salary for the day saying, "I am old; life is more simple for me. You are young, you have to help build a better society, you have to be strong and well-nourished." . . . In Paraiba, Brazil, the communities decided on a day of fasting as a sign of solidarity with the farm workers who had been evicted from the lands where they had worked for decades. On the day of such a fast what would have been eaten is given to the most needy and instead of working for oneself, one works for those who cannot work. "And so, we gathered together in the church very early in the morning to offer our fast. After the offering some went to take food to the poorest families; others expressed their fast by working in the fields of those who were sick. That night we returned to church to complete our fast. The children were there from six to seven; the women from seven to eight and the men from eight until nine o'clock" [Marins, 66].

Uriel Molina describes an action taken by the CEBs in the El Riguero district of Managua in Somoza's time. A characteristic of the CEBs in El Riguero was that some of their members were university students who were trying to live among poor and simple people. Molina writes:

One day . . . it happened that milk had suddenly gone up considerably in price. This situation, which affected the poor, was made the subject of reflection by the community. The university people, following their methods of socio-political analysis, came to the conclusion that this injustice could only be overcome as the poor were made aware of their condition and became organized. Then came the moment of biblical enlightenment. We took 1 Timothy 6:6–10 and 17–19: "Religion, of course, does bring large profits, but only to those who are content with what they have. We brought nothing into the world, and we can take nothing from it; but as long as we have food and clothing, let us be content with that. . . . The love of money is the root of all evils. . . . Warn those who are rich in this world's goods that they are . . . not to set their hopes on money, which is untrustworthy, but on God, who, out of his riches, gives us all that we need for our happiness. Tell them . . . to be generous and willing to share."
    We had to relate our biblical insights to the actual situation. The Bible provided us with the basic impulse, which pushed us into the struggle for the transformation of the existing state of affairs. In order to achieve it, we needed socio-political means. For example, the Bible tells us in the passage quoted: "let us be content with our food and clothing." Our reflection led us to the concept of a new society, where people's primary needs would be satisfied (education for all, food for all, housing for all, health for all). The Bible also says: "tell the rich to be willing to share their goods." Social analysis led us to recognize that society is badly organized, and organized for the benefit of privileged minorities. The

rich needed to be persuaded to change. The conclusion we came to was that they would never do it willingly, and that therefore, if the message was to be effective, it would be necessary to pass through a structural revolution. The meeting finally decided on a concrete symbolic gesture: we would scatter nails along the streets where the milk-lorries would pass, and puncture their tires. The drivers of the vehicles would then be persuaded to allow the young people to distribute the milk to the children. In this way the community meeting was not simply a time of reflection and analysis, but also of organization for the struggle [Molina, 5].

One final example indicates how CEBs, communities of poor people, share the little they have with other communities:

Some communities in Guatemala celebrated a Mass of solidarity with the people of the Church of Nicaragua, which is scarred by the destruction of war. During the offertory, each one placed on the altar his [sic] offering to be sent to this suffering Church. A poor man placed on the altar a small plastic bag containing a handful of beans, nothing else. He was already returning to his place when he stopped. He looked back. Then he went back. He took off his jacket, folded it carefully, affectionately, and left it on the altar with the other offerings. . . . The temperature that evening was 10 degrees Celsius [Marins, 66–67].

It should be clear that the CEB is more than an instrument by which the institutional church reaches and evangelizes the people. The CEB is a new and original way of living Christian faith. It is a new way of organizing the community around the Word of God, around the sacraments, and around new lay ministries (of both men and women). A new distribution of power is evident; the CEB is participatory and avoids all centralization and domination. The CEB is also a place where a true democracy of the people is practiced, where members discuss and decide things together, where critical thought is elicited. Leonardo Boff has written of the CEB that "it makes possible the rise of a rich ecclesial sacramentality. . . . A true 'ecclesiogenesis' is in progress throughout the world, a church being born from the faith of the poor" (L. Boff, 9). The poor, says Boff, is the "new and emerging historical subject which will carry on the Christian project in the world" (L. Boff, 9).

To conclude this section, I should like to quote again from the Puebla final document. The passage may describe best what the CEBs are about. In the preceding section, the bishops are asking when a small community can be considered an authentic CEB. They write:

As a community, the CEB brings together families, adults and young people, in an intimate interpersonal relationship grounded in faith. As an ecclesial reality, it is a community of faith, hope, and charity. It celebrates the Word of God and takes its nourishment from the Eucharist, the culmination of all the sacraments. It fleshes out the commandment of the Lord; and through the service of coordinators, it makes present and operative the mission of the Church and its visible communion with the legitimate pastors. It is a base-level community because it is composed of relatively few members as a permanent body, like a cell of the larger community. "When they deserve their ecclesial designation, they can take charge of their own spiritual and human existence in a spirit of fraternal solidarity" [Third General Conference, 58].[1]

United in a CEB and nurturing their adherence to Christ, Christians strive for a more evangelical way of life amid the people, work together to challenge the egotistical and consumeristic roots of society, and make explicit their vocation to communion with God and their fellow humans. Thus they offer a valid and worthwhile point for building up a new society, "the civilization of love." The CEBs embody the church's preferential love for the common people. In them their religiosity is expressed, valued, and purified; and they are given a concrete opportunity to share in the task of the church and to work committedly for the transformation of the world (Puebla, 641-43).

Analysis of Basic Ecclesial Communities in the Light of Troeltsch's Threefold Typology: Church-Sect-Mysticism

Troeltsch made use of Max Weber's church-sect ideal type construction, but he moved beyond the scope of Weber's twofold typology. He concluded, in *The Social Teaching of the Christian Churches*, that there were *three* forms that the church has taken throughout history in its relationship to the world. Each type is an attempt to combine the two orientations of the gospel: radical *individualism* and *universalism*. The three types are: (1) church; (2) sect; and (3) mysticism. Each one has a distinct Christology, ecclesiology, and social ethic.

Church. This type is best exemplified in the Roman Catholic Church. Troeltsch makes the distinction between pure church type (Roman Catholicism) and church type (ascetic Protestantism). What follows is a description of the pure church type.

    1. Christology —Christ is seen as redeemer.
    2. Ecclesiology —the church is the kingdom of God in the world. It is:
             —a Church of the masses: its standards of entrance are not overwhelmingly high; penance evolved to "keep members in";
             —the extension of the incarnation in history;
             —a highly visible structured entity;
             —hierarchical; contains orders (bishops, priests, deacons);
             —patriarchal;
             —sacramental;
             —it sees redemption for everyone (universalism);
             —a church of saints and sinners;

—perfection is pursued by monastic and religious life (radical individualism).

3. Social Ethic —(view of the world). It is positive toward the world.

—It sees the world as the arena for its ministry and consecration.

—It understands its task as the building of kingdom in every area of life.

—Its view of the state is a positive one.

—It sees itself responsible for the entire society: economy, labor, law, and the family.

—It took the gospel and interpreted it in the light of natural law. It felt the need of more than the biblical ethic with which to act in the world. It, therefore, joined the biblical vision to the philosophical ethic. It saw itself going beyond the biblical vision in order to maintain the biblical vision.

—It adapts itself to the world. Some would say that the price of compromise is too high.

Sect. This type is best exemplified by the Quakers and the Mennonites.

1. Christology —Jesus is the Lord to be imitated. He gives law by which we are to live until he comes again to establish the kingdom. Eschatological view.

2. Ecclesiology —It is a small church.

—It is not for all; it is for an elite who are the elect.

—It does not recruit through baptism; it believes in adult Christianity.

—It is unstructured.

—It is democratic in its proceedings.

—It is a church of saints.

3. Social Ethic —It stands over against the world.

—It withdraws from the world.

—It does not intend to Christianize the whole world.

—It sets up Christian order, based on love, within its own group.

Mysticism. This type is best exemplified in nineteenth-century German piety.

1. Christology —Christ in the Spirit.

2. Ecclesiology —It has no organizational form.

—It is a silent form of Christainity, i.e., not organized.

—Not for the masses.

—It has no role in society; kingdom of God is *only* within us.

3. Social ethic —It has no social teaching, therefore, no social ethic.

In examining the CEBs, it can be said that they have "faith in Jesus" as their motivational force and central to their worship. However, the Jesus worshiped is not only the "risen and exalted Lord"—it is the Jesus in history, the Jesus who walked with and among the poor, healing, feeding, and teaching, the Jesus who announced the arrival of the kingdom of God to the downtrodden, outcasts. CEB members attempt to live the life of that Jesus, doing what he did in their own situation, announcing the kingdom by struggling for justice. They are imbued with his Spirit.

Troeltsch described the church as "an institution . . . able to receive the masses, and to adjust itself to the world, because . . . it can afford to ignore the need of subjective holiness for the sake of the objective treasures of grace and redemption" (Troeltsch, 1960:993).

The CEBs do not see themselves as separate from the masses (the people). They see themselves as the church arising from the people. Although many CEBs are small groups, they are linked to other CEBs and to all other groups in the institutional church. They are "cells of the larger body." However, they do not ignore subjective holiness; grace and redemption are not seen as "objective treasures" dispensed through a sacramental system. They are received through one's action in life with one's community, for others (praxis). Holiness is to be achieved by all in the church, not just by a few (monks and religious), and it is to be achieved by living the gospel which for the CEBs includes "action on behalf of justice and participation in the transformation of the world." These elements are seen as "a constitutive dimension . . . of the Church's mission for the redemption of the human race and its liberation from every oppressive situation" (Bishops' Synod, 4).

The sect, as Troeltsch has described it, is "a voluntary society, composed of strict and definite Christian believers bound to each other by the fact that all have experienced 'the new birth' " (Troeltsch, 1960:993). The CEBs too are voluntary societies. Members make a deliberate choice to be Catholic. Status as a Catholic is no longer inherited; it is achieved through one's own efforts. One participates in the life of the CEB; this is what membership means. All are striving for "the new birth" by the creation of "the new person" for "the new society" (the kingdom of God).

The members of the sect "live apart from the world, are limited to small groups, emphasize the law instead of grace, and . . . set up the Christian order based on love: within their own circle. All is done 'in preparation for and expectation of the coming kingdom of God' " (Troeltsch, 1960:993).

The CEBs are small groups like the sects. Unlike the sects, however, they do not live apart from the world. They are very much engaged in the world through their mode of operation: analyzing their reality, reflection on that reality, movement towards action to correct or enhance their milieu. The CEBs too are preparing for the kingdom of God. But, they see the signs of the kingdom present in what they do together. They are sowing the seeds of the kingdom here and now and perform actions that build up the world so that better signs of the kingdom are present in the here and now. In contrast to the sects, the CEBs are very much this-worldly.

In terms of mysticism, the element that the CEBs have in common is that, as in the Mysticism type, formal worship and doctrine are transformed, but not "into a purely personal and inward experience." The members of the CEBs do experience their faith on a deep, personal level. But, the CEBs are groups whose members live their faith on more than a personal level; the personal experience of faith in Jesus spills over into action to transform their world, and they do this through *collective* action. Their form is permanent, and therefore, "forms of worship, doctrine, and the historical element" are strengthened, not weakened as in the mysticism type.

In order to further compare the CEBs with the church-sect-mysticism types, the Christology, ecclesiology, and social ethic of the CEB will be delineated and compared with the other three.

1. Christology

As Marins has pointed out every ecclesial community ultimately reveals an image of Jesus. That image will determine the ecclesial community's way of being at a specific moment in history and it will determine how the community functions. In other words, "the ecclesial community is the model of the Christology image that she [sic] accepts and manifests" (Marins, 1983:54).

> The CEB in its process of emergence and development lives and transmits an image of Jesus that underlines his presence among and with the poor, announcing the Kingdom of God, denouncing idols, injustices, omissions, and summoning all to construct the true fellowship [sic] befitting the children of God [Marins, 55].

The center of life for the CEB is the person of Jesus Christ. But, there is a new understanding of his life and mission. His life is seen as an expression of fidelity to God and of commitment to humanity within a specific historical context.

The CEBs see Jesus "as the friend who invites us to follow him in community, in a prophetic lifestyle and in a commitment to service of others" (Hennelly, 67).

Comparison

Church. Christ is seen as the redeemer.

Sect. Jesus is the Lord to be imitated. He gives the law by which we are to live until he comes again to establish the kingdom.

Mysticism. Incorporates an eschatological view: Christ in the Spirit.

CEB. Jesus as liberator is seen as present among and with the poor. He announces the kingdom in his historical context, and invites others to follow him in a prophetic lifestyle and in a commitment to service of others in order to further the coming of the kingdom (this-worldly focus).

The sect and the CEB are closest in their imaging of Jesus. Both see him as one to be imitated. However, the CEBs see Jesus to be imitated in announcing the kingdom in their historical context. They collaborate in bringing in the reign of God. This differs from the sect, which waits patiently until Jesus comes to establish the kingdom.

2. Ecclesiology

The CEBs are communities of faith, hope, and love. They are the initial cells of the ecclesial structure and collaborate in the construction of the kingdom of God in their present historical moment. They are a pilgrim people on the march, making history; they are the people of God.

The CEB is not an elite community; it is open to all. However, the CEBs have a particular location—they come from the masses, the poor in Latin America. The CEBs are usually composed of adults.

In the CEBs, those who have had no voice participate in forming the community. All have an equal voice in decision-making, even though each member may be performing different ministries. Structurally, the CEBs are decentralized, nonhierarchical, and communitarian. Operationally, they are nonpatriarchical, democratic, and collegial.

Their goal is universal in that liberation is seen as for everyone. Their starting point is the building of a new society. They play a prophetic role by denouncing injustice and by pointing the way to a new society, one in which the poor will have a place as subjects and not as objects. The CEBs are autonomous units when they are able to have their own ministers and are able to be missionaries to other communities (that is, help new CEBs emerge in other places).

Comparison

Church. Kingdom of God in the world; mass church; highly visible, structured entity; hierarchical; patriarchal; sacramental; redemption for all (universal); church of saints and sinners; perfection not for all, for monastics and religious (radical individualism).

Sect. Small church; for an elite: the elect; adult Christianity; unstructured; nonhierarchical; democratic; church of saints.

Mysticism. No organizational form; silent Christianity.

CEB. The people of God; comes from the masses (the poor); open to all; adult; loose structure; participatory and communitarian; nonhierarchical and decentralized; democratic and collegial; Word of God, central; eucharist celebrated, with song and prayer; liberation for all (universal); church of saints and sinners; prophetic (radical individualism); perfection demanded of all through evangelical living—living the gospel (radical individualism); missionary.

The CEB contains elements of both church and sect in its ecclesiology. It is similar to the church type in that it is structured, although not as highly structured; it is sacramental, but relies heavily on the Word of God, prayer and song, along with the celebration of the eucharist (when possible); it has an orientation toward universalism, although it is liberation as well as redemption that is named here; it too sees itself as a church of saints and sinners; and it captures the element of radical individualism in its prophetic stance and its demand that all live the gospel and struggle for a more just society. Finally, it is open to all.

It is similar to the sect type in that it too is for adults; it is nonhierarchical and democratic. It differs from both the church and sect types in that it originates from among the poor. It is giving rise to a true "ecclesiogenesis," a church born from the faith of the poor. Others who belong to this new church can do so to the degree that they make an option for the poor. In this way, all will work together to build up the kingdom of God, which is a kingdom of peace and love, and most importantly, justice.

The CEB has no elements in common with the mysticism type.

3. Social Ethic

The CEBs see the world as the place where they live out their mission to build up the kingdom. This task is to be accomplished in every area of life: in the church itself and in the society at large.

In Latin America, the CEBs are cognizant of the role that the state plays in the oppression of the people (the poor). The state is seen as presently serving the interests of a small group rather than the interests of the poor majority. They struggle to change this relationship and to place the resources of the State at the service of the people (the poor).

In its method of working (analysis of reality, reflection in faith on social reality, and a commitment to take action), the CEBs search out concrete ways of action that move from a commitment on a local level to the realization of a universal project of liberation. They call for conversion on the personal, family, and group level through a change in fundamental attitudes (egoism, individualism, domination). At the same time, they realize that structural change is needed—action on behalf of justice.

They set up a Christian order, based on love, within their own group and act as leaven in the larger society. However, they do not adapt to the world; they act to change it.

Comparison

Church. Positive attitude toward the world, the arena for its ministry and consecration; positive view of the State; sees itself as responsible for the whole of society; interprets the Gospel in the light of natural law; joins the biblical vision to philosophy; adapts to the world.

Sect. Stands against the world; withdraws from the world; does not intend to Christianize the world; sets up an order, based on love, within its own grouping.

Mysticism. Has no social teaching, therefore, no social ethic.

CEB. Positive attitude toward the world, the arena for its activity and mission; critical view of the present reality of the State, which should change from serving a minority to serving the majority; sees itself as responsible for building the church itself and society at large, in union with others; interprets the gospel in the light of Jesus' action, in love, for justice to the poor; sets up a Christian order, based on love and justice, within its own grouping and acts as a leaven in society at large; acts to change the world.

In terms of its social ethic, the CEB has very little in common with the sect. There is a partial similarity in the kinds of groups the CEB and the sect are. They both set up their groups from the perspective of love. However, the CEB goes beyond the sect in that it joins love to the concrete historical moment through its action for justice. Also, where the sect remains closed in upon itself, the CEB sees itself as opening out to the whole world. As for the mysticism type, the CEB has no elements in common with it, for the mysticism type has no social ethic. The CEB does contain elements of the church type in its social ethic. It is similar to the church type in that it sees its arena for action in the world and not separate from it; it is more critical of the state than is the church type and works with others to make the state more responsive to the poor majority. The CEB not only sees itself as responsible for transforming the society at large but also sees itself as responsible for transforming the church itself.

Where it differs from the church is in its interpretation of the gospel. The CEBs interpret the gospel from the perspective of the poor, not from the perspective of a static reality (natural law). They too have a biblical vision of the kingdom of God, but they do not make use of philosophy to elaborate on it. The CEBs make use of the social sciences, not philosophy. And finally, instead of adapting to the world, the CEBs see as their task to change the world.

Conclusions

The purpose of this chapter was to explore the question: Is the basic ecclesial community a new type of religious social organization that follows from the response of Christian faith in Latin America to the modern world, or is it of the church, sect, or mysticism type? In order to answer this question, CEBs were defined and their actions delineated. They were then analyzed in the light of Troeltsch's threefold typology—church/sect/ mysticism— according to the categories of (1) Christology, (2) ecclesiology, and (3) social ethic.

Based on this research, my conclusion is that the CEB is a new type of religious social organization that follows from the response of Christian faith in Latin America to the modern world. The CEBs are neither church nor sect, as defined by Troeltsch, but rather are ecclesial units which join the structure of the sect (radical individualism) with the charism and commitment of the church (universalism). They are imbued with the Spirit of Jesus who is their motivating force and whose mission to proclaim and realize the kingdom of God is their own.[2]

Since the CEBs emerged, their impact has been enormous on the church and on other sectors of society. For the church, they have meant movement/

participation by the grassroots—by the poor. They signal the beginning of a change in the medieval structure of the Roman church from a hierarchical mode of being to one that is communal and truly of the people. The change has not been finalized. Like the CEBs themselves, it is in process, a process that begins from the bottom, so to speak, and includes all who join with the poor in the historical project of liberation. This dynamic process has been captured in the concepts of "the Church born from the people" or "the Church born from the poor." These are not just words but point to a whole new model of church being born, a whole new way of being church. The building blocks of this new church are the CEBs.[3]

For example, Aloisio Lorscheider, the archbishop of Fortaleza, Brazil, has written of the transformation in his ministry and lifestyle:

> Soon after coming to Fortaleza, in August 1973, I began to experience a change in how I saw the episcopal ministry. In the South . . . I had been far more the person who teaches what he knows, without any great concern for the problems . . . affecting the poor. It was a simple transmission of a store of knowledge, leaving the people to decide how it could be applied to their lives. . . . I was more of a teacher and president of the liturgy than a real evangelizer within the actual experience of the people.
>
> In Fortaleza, in contact with another type of . . . community . . . my episcopal ministry, in its triple function of teaching, sanctifying and governing, began to take on a different aspect. . . .
>
> The fact of being new to the region . . . meant that I had to listen in order to find out what was really going on. . . . This listening soon became something more. It became a habit, a discovery that led to a complete change in me and my ministry.
>
> The people . . . were communicating not knowledge, but experience, a way of life that could be glimpsed, a life of faith with deep roots in reality. . . .
>
> In a short while it became clear to me that my episcopal ministry would be exercised in a different way. I would always be an extra member of a community, with my own special responsibility in it, but without seeing myself or being seen as the head of that community, as superior to it; rather . . . I should be there only to serve at the moment when they felt a need for the service I could give, or when I felt, in the spirit of love, that I could be a help to them on their way. I was no longer the teacher or instructor, but one animator among a lot of other animators. I too had to become a pupil before thinking of being a master. But I no longer see myself as a master, because there is only one Master. I think of myself far more as being a disciple, with them, of the Master, listening to Jesus and his Spirit, attentive with the whole community to what Jesus and the Spirit have to say to the Church. . . .
>
> Finally, this new way of being a bishop based on very concrete contact with the communities of poor believers leads the bishop to a simpler

life-style, making him feel the need to identify himself more and more with Christ present in the poor, avoiding anything that can give an impression of grandeur or control. In this way the bishop continues to be transformed into one more brother within a community of brothers and sisters [Lorscheider, 47–49].

Lorscheider's testimony is indicative of what is taking place within the Latin American church today. The poor are evangelizing the church. This does not signify just a new day for the church: It signifies a whole new way of being church.

In the 1950s, the Latin American church had been concerned with its waning influence both on the larger society and on its own members. In the early 1900s, Troeltsch too had been concerned about the ability of the churches—both Roman Catholic and Protestant—to influence modern society as they had done in the past. They "have spent their force," he declared. He concluded that a new kind of Church was needed, one which would "reconcile these three sociological groupings [church, sect, mysticism] within the same structure" (Troeltsch, 1960, 1012).

I submit that the CEBs point to this new model of church; they point the way to such a synthesis. The CEBs are the church influencing society in a radically new way: from the masses, the poor, the marginalized. They have given voice to those who have had no voice—in the church or in the larger society. And they are emerging at a time when the poor are irrupting into history all over the globe, when they are making themselves known and heard in places like El Salvador, Nicaragua, South Africa, and the Philippines.

Further, the CEBs are developing a whole new generation of leaders in Latin America. One author has noted:

> These skills can be transferred, for the most part, to other spheres. Thus the ability to think on one's feet, to lead discussions, to take positions and defend them, to attempt community problem-solving, to act as advocates or mediators, or to administer larger social units than the family—all these are skills that can be applied directly in the political arena. The existence of such resources on a widespread basis means a new day is dawning for the church [Cleary, 117].

This new day is not without suffering. It is being born at great sacrifice and loss of life. For the emergence of the poor as an organized group has threatened those in power and their reaction has been brutal as the poor people have organized to claim their human rights and dignity. The Latin American church has become a church of martyrs and many of these martyrs come from the CEBs. Leonardo Boff writing in *Church: Charisma and Power*, the book that resulted in his being silenced by Rome, says of these times:

> We are living in privileged times. There is an upsurge of life in the Church that is revitalizing the entire body from head to toe. The Church has been

placed on the road to renewal, which will surely result in a new manifestation of the Church as institution. There are powerful and living forces, particularly at the grass roots, that are not sufficiently recognized by the traditional channels of the Church's present organization. The grass roots are asking for a new structure, a new ecclesial division of labor and of religious power. For this, a new vision of the Church is necessary. This vision has not yet been developed systematically in a way that responds to the demands of our global reality, but it is necessary given what is happening in Latin America and elsewhere in the world [L. Boff, ix].

The bishops at Puebla saw these communities as "the hope of the future." Within the CEBs lies not only the vision of a new church, but also the vision of a new society, one of peace, love and justice. And this is possible because "a true 'ecclesiogenesis' is in progress throughout the world, a Church being born from the faith of the poor" (L. Boff, 9).

Notes

1. The quotation here is taken from the exhortation by Pope Paul VI, *Evangelii Nuntiandi* (*Evangelization in the Modern World*). This was written in 1975 after the Bishops' Synod of 1974 could not come up with a document that all could agree on. Paul took the materials from the Synod and wrote the encyclical.

Father Gerard Cambron, a Canadian priest who worked many years in Brazil, has said that a group is an autonomous church when it is able to have its own ministers and able to be missionary to other communities. Barbara English believes that Cambron was using the term "base community" as early as 1958. Cambron had gone to Honduras in the early 1960's and was probably there at the time when "Delegates of the Word" were being trained there. When he turned to Brazil, he became director of Illich's language school in Rio where he influenced many missionaries who came there on their way to their missions, particularly in northeast Brazil (English, Interview).

2. I use the word "units" here instead of "church," to avoid confusion. However, it is clear from my analysis and from that of others that the CEBs are church at the local level.

3. Additional research to further support my conclusions would be to look specifically at the "church of the poor" and its impact on the Latin American church and society. Another piece that needs further work is the link to Troeltsch's mysticism type. There is a Spirit that motivates the CEBs and its dynamism moves people to action.

References

Adams, James Luther. 1982. "Foreword," in Robert J. Rubanowice, *Crisis in Consciousness: The Thought of Ernst Troeltsch*. Tallahassee: University Presses of Florida.

Bainton, Roland H. April 1951. "Ernst Troeltsch—Thirty Years Later," *Theology Today*, vol. 8, 70-96.

Barreiro, Alvaro. 1982. *Basic Ecclesial Communities: The Evangelization of the Poor*. Maryknoll, NY: Orbis.

Berryman, Phillip. 1984. *The Religious Roots of Rebellion*. Maryknoll, NY: Orbis.

Betto, Frei. 1979. *Puebla para o Povo*. Petrópolis, Brazil: Vozes.

Bishops' Synod. 1971. *Justice in the World*. Boston: St. Paul Editions.

Boff, Clodovis. 1981. "The Nature of Basic Christian Communities." *Concilium*, no. 144: 54–58.

Boff, Leonardo. 1985. *Church: Charisma and Power*. New York: Crossroad.

Boff, Leonardo, and Virgil Elizondo, eds. 1984. "The People of God Amidst the Poor," *Concilium*, no. 176.

Bruneau, Thomas C. 1974. *The Political Transformation of the Brazilian Catholic Church*. New York: Cambridge University Press.

Cleary, Edward L. 1985. *Crisis and Change*. Maryknoll, NY: Orbis.

Comblin, José. 1975. "As comunidades de base como lugar de experiencias novas," *Concilium*, no. 104, 457, quoted in Alvaro Barreiro, *Basic Ecclesial Communities*.

Di Carlo, Liz. 1982. "The Catholic Church and Revolutionary Struggle in Central America"(unpublished paper).

Elizondo, Virgil, and Norbert Greinacher, eds. 1981. "Tensions Between the Churches of the First World and the Third World," *Concilium*, vol. 144.

English, Barbara. 1985. *Until the Song Is Sung*. Brazil: Sisters of Notre Dame.

————. January, 1985. Interview.

Hennelly, Alfred T. 1983. "Grassroots Communities: A New Model of Church," in James E. Hug, ed., *Tracing the Spirit*. New York: Paulist, 60-82.

Heilbroner, Robert L. 1974. *An Inquiry into the Human Prospect*. New York: Norton.

Hug, James E., ed. 1983. *Tracing the Spirit*. New York: Paulist.

Institute for Central American Studies. August 1985. "Challenge to the Past—Thrust into the Future: Vatican II ('62-'65)," in *Mesoamerica,* vol. 4, no. 8, 2-3.

Kirby, Peadar, and David J. Molineaux. June 1985. "CEBs Promote New Ministries, New Model of Church," *Latinamerica Press*, vol. 17, no. 24.

Lorscheider, Aloisio. 1984. "The Re-defined Role of the Bishop in a Poor, Religious People (Meio Popular Pobre e Religioso)," *Concilium*, no. 176, 47–49.

Marins, José. 1983. *Basic Ecclesial Communities: The Church From the Roots*. Quezon City, Philippines: Claretian Publications.

Míguez Bonino, José. 1983. *Toward a Christian Political Ethics*. Philadelphia: Fortress.

Molina Oliu, Uriel. 1984. "How a People's Christian Community (Comunidad Cristiana Popular) Is Structured and How It Functions." *Concilium*, no. 176, 3-9.

Morgan, Robert, and Michael Pye, eds. 1977. *Ernst Troeltsch: Writings on Theology and Religion*. Atlanta: John Knox.

Pironio, Eduardo F. 1970. "Christian Interpretation of the Signs of the Times in Latin America Today," in Second General Conference of Latin American Bishops, *The Church in the Present Day Transformation of Latin America in the Light of the Council*, vol. 1. Washington, DC: United States Catholic Conference, 107–28.

Reist, Benjamin A. 1966. *Toward a Theology of Involvement*. Philadelphia: Westminster.

Rubanowice, Robert J. 1982. *Crisis in Consciousness: The Thought of Ernst Troeltsch*. Tallahassee: University Presses of Florida.

Second General Conference of Latin American Bishops. 1970. *The Church in the Present-Day Transformation of Latin America in the Light of the Council*, vol. 1. Washington, DC: United States Catholic Conference.

Sleigh, R. S. 1923. *The Insufficiency of Christianity*. London: James Clarke and Company.

Third General Conference of Latin American Bishops. 1979. *Evangelization at Present and in the Future of Latin America*, vol. 2, Conclusions. Washington, DC: United States Catholic Conference.

Troeltsch, Ernst. 1960. *The Social Teaching of the Christian Churches*. Chicago: University of Chicago Press.

———. 1971. *The Absoluteness of Christianity and the History of Religions*. Richmond, VA: John Knox.

Zenteno, Arnoldo. March/April 1982. "Basic Ecclesial Communities in the Popular Church," *Ladoc*, vol. 12, no. 4, 14–20.

CHAPTER 9

Indigenization of the Christian Faith in Cameroon

Festus A. Asana

The Republic of Cameroon has often been described as Africa in miniature, and rightly so. Located in the heart of Africa, Cameroon has almost every physical feature one will find anywhere on that continent. Covering an area of 475,000 square kilometers (about the size of the state of California) and located between the Tropic of Cancer and the Equator, Cameroon opens onto the Atlantic Ocean and stretches from rain forests through thick grasslands to Sahel savannahs. The highest mountain in West Africa (Mount Cameroon) and the second most rainy spot in the world (Dubunscha) are in Cameroon. There are two distinct seasons, the rainy season, which covers about two-thirds of the year (March to October), and the dry season.

Culturally, Cameroon is equally varied. Latest statistics show that there are about two hundred nineteen languages and dialects in the country and this shows the cultural diversity among Cameroon's ten million people. As one travels throughout the country, one can notice the richness of Cameroonian culture in the traditional architecture, the songs and dances, the attire, the food, and the customs.

Politically, the Republic of Cameroon prides itself on being one of the most peaceful and developed countries on the continent of Africa. Completely surrounded by neighboring countries which have had bloody coups d'etat, Cameroon stands like an island of peace in the midst of chaos. It has a democratic system of government with an elected president as head of state, a national assembly, and one political party. Because of its stability, avenues of cooperation and development have opened up with the outside world.

With its central position on the map of Africa linking the western, eastern, northern, and southern parts of the vast continent, Cameroon has become the center of numerous international conferences and foreign investments. It is the only country in Africa with English and French as the two official languages. The country's economy is growing steadily and life expectancy is 46.9 years for men, and 50.1 years for women. There are about twelve thousand people per medical doctor. The literacy rate is one of the highest in Africa. The struggle continues in this prosperous nation to fight inflation, improve road networks, medical services, and achieve equitable distribution of wealth and total unity.

Cameroon also has the traditional history of migrations, and resettlements characteristic of other countries in earlier centuries. Its later political history is a record of colonizations and foreign interference. Today that history is still unfolding in an era of independence as the nation strives to assert itself in the African continent's political arena and the world at large.

The peace and progress of Cameroon have often been attributed to good leadership and religion. There is freedom of worship. Statistics indicate that about 35 percent of the population is Roman Catholic, 18 percent Protestant, 22 percent Muslim, and 25 percent African Traditional Religion, all these religious groups coexisting peacefully. The work of the Christian churches in the development of Cameroon cannot be overemphasized.

Perhaps one of the earliest pieces of information recorded on Cameroonian contact with the rest of the world is an inscription on a metal plate found in a Carthaginian temple. It reveals that Carthaginian sailors, under the leadership of Hanno, the son of Hamilcar, visited the coast of Cameroon in about 500 BCE. The record states that from a mountain, which the inhabitants called the mountain of God, came fiery floods emanating great heat (Keller, 1). This was Mount Cameroon in volcanic eruption, which Hanno described: "we saw it at night, a land full of fire. In the middle was a lofty fire larger than all the rest touching seemingly the stars" (Neba, 2).

It is not until 1472 that further contacts were made with Europe when Fernando Po, the Portuguese navigator, arrived on an island thirty-five kilometers off the coast of Cameroon and gave his name to it. Later on, Portuguese traders came to Cameroon and, finding many prawns in the estuary of the Wouri, named it *Rio dos Camerões* (River of Prawns). *Camerones*, the Spanish version of *Camerões*, later gave birth to the name of the country, Cameroons (now the Republic of Cameroon).

Prior to the European colonization, the final partition of the continent of Africa in the nineteenth century, and the creation of the present state of Cameroon, there existed several small, independent kingdoms with well-established local governments. Each grouping had its political setup with respected chiefs, counselors, and family heads. Ethnic groups encountered one another through trade, rarely through intermarriage, and often in wars.

Colonization accompanied Christian missions, which often clashed with existing local religious practices. Before the coming of Christianity, African Traditional Religion existed in various forms in Cameroon as in the rest of what the European world referred to as the Dark Continent. In most cases, the chief of an ethnic group was also the chief priest during religious sacrifices and other ceremonies. My use of the past tense does not imply the total elimination of traditional systems. Even with the popularity of Christianity and Islam and the strong influence of European customs, traditional Cameroonian ways of life and religious practices are very evident as one travels from one region to the other.

Early European explorers and missionaries, referring to these traditional systems, used pejorative terms like primitive, savage, uncivilized, uncultured, and backward. Lugira observes the following on the issue of the misrepresentation of African Traditional Religion:

> Since the medieval times a host of travellers have extensively waded through and along some parts of the African continent. However effectively, it was during the nineteenth century that travellers could claim to have penetrated the interior parts of black Africa. Travellers on their return from Africa back to Europe have written accounts which have greatly influenced the understanding of African Religion by Western peoples. . . . It is from such travellers' descriptions that Western influence of African Religion have reduced that religion to nothing but superstition, grigris, juju, witchcraft, sorcery, fetishism [Lugira, 12].

Idowu has also pointed out several of the errors made about Africa, its people, culture, and religion (see Idowu, 1973). While complete accuracy cannot be claimed on the religious state of African countries like Cameroon before the coming of European Christian missionaries, many good records are available and old religious practices continue today in various forms and places, despite foreign interference. John Mbiti has compiled some findings on the African religious heritage of which Cameroon is part. In the different African cultures, the idea of God and the existence of that spiritual realm is unquestionable, even if interpretations and practices may be different. On the worship of God, Mbiti states:

> In many and various ways, African people respond to their spiritual world of which they are sharply aware. This response generally takes on the form of worship which is internalised in different acts and sayings. These acts may be formal or informal, regular or extempore, communal or individual, ritual or unceremonial, through word or deed. They vary from one society to another, and from one area to another [Mbiti, 58].

As one travels through Cameroon from north to south, this religious variety can be noticed in various forms even today. The situation today points to a religious heritage that existed long before the arrival of the Christian church. A religion existed; Africans were introduced to Christianity, not to God, as missionaries often claimed.

Until a few years ago, Alfred Saker, an English Baptist pastor, was popularly regarded as the first Christian missionary to Cameroon. But it is now clear that the Rev. Joseph Merrick, a black Baptist and freed slave from Jamaica, was the pioneer who initiated a Christian mission to Cameroon. Leaving his large parish in Jericho, Jamaica, Joseph Merrick decided to go back to his roots and share the good news of Jesus Christ. Joined by Rev. Alfred Saker and Dr. Prince in England, they traveled with their wives to Clarence in Spanish-occupied Fernando Po in 1843. They were also accompanied by over forty people, including children, most of them blacks, some going as missionaries and others as settlers.

After making some contact trips to the coast of Cameroon from Clarence, Joseph Merrick finally settled in Bimbia in 1844 and opened a mission station there. On June 10, 1845, Alfred Saker arrived in Douala, a main coastal kingdom. Three years later he opened a school. Because of persecution on the island of Fernando Po, Saker in 1858 transferred the Christian colony from the island to the mainland. Alfred Saker goes down in the history of the church in Cameroon as one of the most zealous pioneers. He taught the natives various crafts, learned the Douala language, and translated the Bible into that language. On February 23, 1872, the entire Douala Bible was printed with the help of the printing press which friends had sent from Scotland and Norfolk.

With ruined health after years of hard work, Alfred Saker left Africa for the last time in November 1876, after bringing another English pastor to continue the work. He died on March 13, 1880. In his last public speech, to delegates of the home churches in Glasgow, he said:

> If the African is a brother, should we not give him some of our bread and a draught of our water? Oh that I have another life to go out there. The field is white there and the multitudes are in darkness still [Keller, 6].

Meanwhile Joseph Merrick had started printing the Gospel of Matthew, Genesis, and Bible stories in the Isubu language. He also helped to train villagers in practical work. He fell seriously ill and left Africa on October 22, 1849, having been succeeded by another missionary. Joseph Merrick died aboard the ship before he could reach Jamaica. Several other missionaries have their graves on the coast of Cameroon, the climate and lack of adequate medical facilities being the main cause and malaria being the greatest killer.

We notice in the cases of the two pioneer missionaries that from the onset they tried to make the gospel relevant to the people to whom they witnessed. By translating the Bible, they made God's word accessible in indigenous languages. Teaching the people crafts and other skills in homes and schools, living with the people in humble and sometimes difficult conditions, were all powerful ways of identifying with the people and preaching by example. The gospel did not only speak but acted.

The spread of the gospel inland encountered several difficulties, some of them political and others religious. Some of the African chiefs felt that their authority as religious and political sovereigns was threatened. They resisted the missionaries at first. In some cases, the missionaries are said to have been feared as powerful wizards.

External political forces greatly affected the spread of Christianity during those early years. Alfred Saker had created a Christian colony in a coastal town he named Victoria (now Lembe), but with the coming of the English, Germans, and French, who ruled different parts of Cameroon at different times, Christian missionary control was forced to correspond with the sovereign country. One example is the reason for Alfred Saker's leaving Fernando Po with his following. When Spain took control of the island, the following proclamation sent Saker away:

Don Carlos Chacón, Knight of the Military Order of San Hermengildo, Captain of Frigate in the Spanish Navy, Commander of HER CATHO-LIC MAJESTY's Squadron in the Islands of Fernando Po, Annobon, and Corisco, Governor General of all the said Islands, etc., makes known to all,

1. The religion of the colony is that of the Roman Catholic Church as the only one in the Kingdom of Spain, with the exclusion of any other; and no other religious profession [is] tolerated or allowed, but that made by the missionaries of the afore-said Catholic religion.

2. Those who profess any other religion which be not the Catholic should confine their worship within their own private houses or families and limit it to the members thereof [Keller, 3].

As early as 1884, the Christian church in Cameroon began to function under different denominational names. With the annexation of Cameroon by Germans, the Basel Mission, a Swiss-German Evangelical missionary society, stepped in and made arrangements to continue the work of the English Baptists who had to leave. Soon there were three Christian missionary traditions represented in Cameroon—Baptist, Presbyterian, and Catholic—each vying for the control of a reasonable area and population.

It is interesting how the political annexation by the Germans took place. A few days before Hewett, a British consul in Nigeria, arrived with authority from the foreign secretary in England to sign treaties of annexation and trade with Cameroon chiefs, the German flag was flying in Douala. Three Douala chiefs had signed the following agreement with German traders following the arrival of Dr. Nachtigal, the German consul general at Tunis, who had been instructed by Chancellor Bismarck to go and supervise the situation in Cameroon:

We the undersigned, independent kings and chiefs of the Cameroons on the Cameroon River, which country is bounded by the River Kimbia in the North, by the River Kwa Kwa in the South and extends to four degrees ten minutes Northern Latitude, have resolved out of our own free will today in a meeting in the German factory King Akwa Strand as follows: "With this day we transfer our sovereign rights, the legislation and the administration of the country completely to the gentlemen Eduard Schmidt and Johannes Voss as representatives of the commercial houses Wormann, Jantzen and Thormahlen in Hamburg, which trade on this river many years. We have transferred our commercial laws, the legislation and the administration to the said firms—"[Keller, 9].

It is after such political and commercial openings were made that missionaries also came in, sometimes viewed by the natives as part of the colonial authorities, until their mission was clarified through the preaching of the gospel. Courageous as they were in breaking new ground by going into new and strange areas, they certainly needed some political security, which their home government provided indirectly through the presence of their representatives. It is not true, in every case, however, that the missionary and the trader or colonial master agreed on what they were out for, but in most cases they facilitated each other's work, having generally the same superiority complex toward the native Cameroonians and their culture.

Unlike the political colonial authorities, whose primary aim was commerical exploitation, the missionaries made an effort to train some Cameroonians early enough to cooperate with them in the preaching of the gospel. Between the two world wars, when the German and Swiss missionaries were forced to leave Cameroon, the churches found themselves in great need of leadership for most of the workers had been dependent on them. The few Cameroonian ministers, like Johanes Ekese, Modi Din, John Ashili—suddenly found themselves faced with the task of covering vast distances to baptize new Christians and strengthen the churches. After the two world wars, with the changing of the political scene in Cameroon, missionary work was intensified from different angles. While most Christian missions moved from the coast northward, Islam spread from the northern part of the country, having come from North Africa through the Sahara desert. Some of the Christian missions included the Basel Mission, the American Presbyterian Mission, the Paris Mission, the Norwegian Mission, the Sudan interior Mission, the Roman Catholic Mission, and some Pentecostal groups, which followed much later. Each of these looked up to European or American headquarters for directions in their development. Sometimes the competitive spirit was unhealthy and was a counterwitness to the gospel instead of the good example that was supposed to be set.

While the Christian missionary churches deserved praise for pioneering formal Western education through the opening of schools and the introduction of development projects, missionaries still held to leadership roles and did not quickly foresee their replacement by Cameroonians. This lack of foresight differed from one missionary group to another, as the granting of autonomy to Cameroonian church leaders later showed. Schools, medical centers, and church headquarters were all under the direction of missionaries, who also controlled all finances. This in some cases gave place to the false accusation that Christianity was the white people's religion. The churches and their related institutions were run according to the dictates of the missionaries, sometimes at the displeasure of their Cameroonian counterparts, who generally had little or no voice.

The year 1957 was of historic importance for the three largest Protestant missions in Cameroon. The Presbyterian Church in Cameroon (from the Basel Mission in the English-speaking western region), the Eglise Presbytérienne Camerounaise (from the American Presbyterian Mission in the French-speaking region), and the Eglise Evangélique du Cameroun (from the Paris Mission) all became autonomous the same year. In some cases strong friction between missionaries and local church leaders came to the surface, betraying the dictatorial and unyielding attitude of some missionaries.

Coming three years before the birth of the Republic of Cameroon, the independence of these three churches was a leading example in the direction of autonomy and indigenization. The independence of these churches did not mean the dismissal of all foreign personnel and cooperation, for as long as the Christian church exists, wherever its communities may be, there has to be interdependence among its members. Fraternal workers, as they are now called, continue to serve from former missionary bodies in Cameroonian churches.

Taking the example of the Presbyterian Church in Cameroon, the process of autonomy was very systematic and gradual. Following the taking over of the churches by Cameroonians in 1957, the schools were transferred in 1966, and finally, on April 28, 1968, there was the total integration of the rest of the property (lands, medical institutions, etc.) into African ownership. Let it be noted here that some missionaries in the different denominations mourned the loss of their control over the Cameroonian church, institutions, and property, and some Cameroonians also dreaded the takeover, fearing that the glorious days of the church would also go with the departure of the missionaries. Since there had been independence all along, some minds had been tuned in that direction, resulting in a lack of courage and confidence in indigenization. The then moderator of the Presbyterian Church in Cameroon, the Rt. Rev. J. C. Kangsen, expressed the importance of the handing-over event in the following words:

> It has happened. And glory be to God. History has been made today in the Federal Republic of Cameroon, a new milestone has been reached in the history of the Presbyterian Church in West Cameroon. You have all seen what has happened—the Basel Mission has transferred to the church all institutions the mission built up for so many years. What does this signify? For us it means several things of great importance. . . . This event first of all, signifies that the Basel Mission has fully fulfilled its duty, namely the preaching of the Gospel, establishing churches, training local leadership in the churches and finally handing over the church and all the responsibility to the indigenous people. Secondly it corrects Cam-

eroonian thinking. For a long time it was thought that the church was an affair of the white man . . . by handing over the church and its institutions to Cameroonian leadership the Basel Mission has, by this act, shown that God has black angels and black saints in our church [Keller, 140].

The process of indigenization of the church in Cameroon has not been a bed of roses but it has not been without hope either. While the missionaries had made some effort in training personnel, the autonomous churches needed to precipitate the training of more people to take up responsibilities in different institutions of the church. The hospitals, agricultural centers, schools, handicraft centers, and other wings of the churches had been started as ways of witnessing practically to the loving care of Christ's good news and these had to be continued. Despite the idea of the disrespect of prophets in their own home (Mark 6:4; Luke 4:24), there was also the aspect of identifying better with one's own kind.

Priority has been given to evangelization, as recorded during the silver jubilee celebration of the Presbyterian Church in 1982:

After 1957, the young church had to face the problem of development, personnel, social engagement, etc., with evangelism being top on the list. Almost every consultation that has been held in the church has concluded that evangelism is the prime task of the church. In this connection sufficient stress has been laid on evangelism as the proclamation of the whole Gospel of each cultural, social, economic and political context [Nyansako-ni-Nku, 13].

Since independence, many new congregations have been opened by the different churches, and Cameroonians can hear the gospel preached in their own languages by their own people. Efforts have been made to indigenize the liturgies as much as possible, but there is still a long way to go. Many native Cameroonian musical instruments, which in the past were detested as pagan, are today used freely in the churches for the glory of God. Many songs for worship have been composed in Cameroonian languages with native rhythms. Thought has been given to the architecture of church buildings, trying to erect buildings that identify with local structures and reflect the culture of the people. Instead of church bells imported from Europe, local churches have beautifully sounding wooden drums to call people to worship.

A classic example that has become a great attraction is a Catholic church in the capital city of Yaoundé that has become popularly referred to as "the dancing church." Located in a section of the city known as Njong Melen, the church has only a little shade over the altar and mass is held in the open air surrounded by houses. A good part of the mass is dancing to the rhythm of Cameroonian singing and drumming. The offering is in cash and kind, and the priests lead the mass entirely in Ewondo, a Cameroonian language. It is a magnificent sight.

In the process of indigenization, the question has always been how to make the Christian faith more relevant to the average Cameroonian. The total solution is not a one-day computer matter. Obstacles stand in the way of the church in Cameroon, just as they have always obstructed the Christian faith throughout history in various ways. Some who have made their living by crooked ways, cheating others, would love to see the church go away, since it threatens their falsehood. In some areas, some Cameroonians are so attached to the traditional religious practices of their ancestors that they have nothing to do with Christianity since they too are worshiping God in their own way.

With local church seminaries in the hands of Cameroonian teachers now, orientations are different. Although there is still considerable reference to European theology, practical Cameroonian issues and matters of the Christian faith can be discussed and appreciated out of experience. Many programs have been revised to reflect the African context and local situations, especially in the field of practical theology.

Some of the issues that made Christianity appear foreign to Cameroonians were:

1. The gospel was brought by strange people from an unknown part of the world.
2. Missionaries accompanied oppressive political agents who exploited the people culturally and economically, leaving them suspicious.
3. Missionaries did not identify with Cameroonians culturally and linguistically.
4. Missionaries tended to dictate to Cameroonians, despising their viewpoint and way of life as inferior.
5. Missionaries came with the wrong notion that Black Africans had no meaningful religion and had no belief in God.
6. Missionaries did not trust or respect Cameroonians to whom they preached the gospel.
7. Missionaries tried to separate people from their families by preaching segregation and building Christian colonies.
8. Sometimes the missionaries' way of life was incompatible with the gospel they preached to others.

Although these and other points did not apply to all missionaries or at all times, they were often generalized. Most missionaries were genuine, committed in their mission and sincere as they came out to Africa, but they were also honestly wrong in certain aspects of their worldview and conceptions. The result was the weakening of the foundation of the very house they were struggling to build. For many Cameroonians, the gospel remained superficial and out of context.

While a lot of effort has been made to indigenize the Christian faith in Cameroon since the end of the traditional foreign missionary enterprise, I find a number of avenues in which effort and radical changes need to be made.

The structures of the present autonomous churches in Cameroon were organized by missionaries. Sometimes stipulations in local church constitutions do not quite fit local situations. Unfortunately, most of these things have not been changed: Cameroonians lack the courage to experiment with new ideas more in tune with their local needs. Many items in our church constitutions need to be changed to face realities of the Cameroonian context.

We need theologies that are not just reflections of European and American experience but of the gospel as speaking directly to the Cameroonian situation. Some theological issues which may shake Europe, may not have the same impact in a local village in Cameroon. Cameroonian Christian theologians need to think seriously about what we can learn from Western theology and what the West can learn from us, examining critically issues like polygamy and secret societies in joint projects.

Practically, because of the economic changes, Cameroonian churches are running into financial problems, facing the threat of having to close some institutions that have been very helpful to the community and having their pastors deprived of reasonably adequate material support. This threat has also resulted in a drop in the number and quality of students admitted in the local seminaries. The pattern of church personnel and support will need to be examined to see what changes could be made to improve the situation. Perhaps the patterns inherited from missionaries cannot quite fit our situation. In worship, most of the liturgies are still heavily Western despite the few indigenous items introduced. Vestments, hymnals, and whole liturgies reflect forms more European than Cameroonian. How well does the *Book of Common Order* written for use in the Church of England, or *The Church Hymnary* written for the Presbyterian churches in Scotland, England, and Australia, fit in a worship service in Cameroon?

I saw snow for the first time when I left Africa, but years back in Cameroon, during our dry and brown, dusty Christmas season, we would sing:

> In the bleak mid-Winter,
> Frosty wind made moan,
> Earth stood hard as iron,
> Water like a stone;
> Snow had fallen, snow on snow,
> Snow on snow,
> In the bleak mid-winter
> Long ago [*Church Hymnary*, 17].

Divisive attitudes of competing churches are a scandal and do not speak well of the love that Christianity is out to preach. Traditional Cameroonian societies have family and communities as priorities, so a united front presented by the church would be more appealing and would identify well with the indigenization process of the Christian faith.

The churches need to continue to put into practice the emphasis laid on evangelism, changing some of the patterns and attitudes of a superiority complex in the church. Rather than scramble to take over the places and positions of foreign missionaries, the Cameroonian churches have the task of going out to continue witnessing in other ways.

Lastly, someone has said that the two greatest things we can give our children are roots and wings. While the Cameroon churches are pressing forward to indigenize and to grow in every way, they must not lose sight of the many roots from which they sprang both as Africans and as part of the universal church family, continuing on the foundation laid by missionaries. To this, we turn to Lamin Sanneh who advises:

> The role of the missionary needs to be investigated for the light it may throw on the whole issue of indigenization. We would need to know more than pronouncements made from different ideological positions. It may often be the case that the missionary has stood in the way of indigenization, either deliberately or unwittingly. But it may happen that the missionary facilitates indigenization, not only by his linguistic labours but by the attention he allows local Christians to pay to certain cultural themes, such as hymns and sacred songs in the writing down of local stories, myths, and folklore. Even the notion of looking to the past age of the church is capable of stimulating an enhanced apprehension of the African sacred past. Sometimes, indeed, it is this prior sense of the sacred past which attunes the African to the message of Christianity [Sanneh, 246–47].

As for the clear direction and destiny of the process of indigenization of the Christian faith in Cameroon, we cannot determine it at this time. With the changing of time, the understanding of indigenization may also change and only posterity will be in the position to fully evaluate the effectiveness, purpose, and ineffectiveness of the process now in progress.

References

Church Hymnary, The. 1927. London: Oxford University Press.

Idowu, E. Bolagi. 1973. *African Traditional Religion, A Definition.* Maryknoll, NY: Orbis.

Keller, Werner. 1969. *The History of the Presbyterian Church in West Cameroon.* Victoria: Pres Book Printing.

Lugira, Aloysius Muzzuganda. 1981. *African Religion, A Prolegomenal Essay on the Emergence and Meaning of African Autochthonous Religions.* Roxbury: Omenana.

Mbiti, John S. 1969. *African Religions and Philosophy*. New York: Praeger.
Neba, Aaron. 1982. *Modern Geography of the United Republic of Cameroon*. Rensse-
    laer.
Nyansako-ni-Nku, ed. 1982. *Journey in Faith; The Story of the Presbyterian Church in
    Cameroon*. Presbyterian Church in Cameroon.
Sanneh, Lamin. 1983. *West African Christianity: The Religious Impact*. Maryknoll,
    NY: Orbis.

PART FIVE

IN THE UNITED STATES

CHAPTER 10

Contextualizing the Faith: The African-American Tradition and Martin Luther King, Jr.

Preston N. Williams

It is often the case that new concepts point to occurrences, phenomena, or events that are familiar and ordinary once they have been described. The new ordering or labeling frequently does not uncover an unknown something, but rather reveals a depth or richness to be found in the known and commonplace that one experiences in a fresh and creative way. Something like this is conveyed by the phrase "contextualizing the faith." This is a process that has occurred in the past, is occurring now, and will continue to occur in the future; yet it is seldom identified, isolated, and studied—because of its very ordinariness. Contextualizing takes place in every form of faith, Christian or non-Christian, liberal or conservative, revolutionary or nonrevolutionary. Contemporary usage of the phrase is apt and good because it is wise in these times of change to remind all believers that their faith is never free from the earthen vessels of culture, class, gender, race, and the multitude of factors present in their natures and environments. To say this, however, is not to say that a particular form of the faith is inauthentic or relative, but only that it has no privileged status in respect to truth, whether it be recognized as orthodox, mainline, popular, or indigenous. Whether true or false it participates in the process of contextualization. Truth is present when the nature of the faith and contextualization correspond with that which is ultimate reality.

To speak, then, of the contextualization of the African-American version of the Christian faith is not necessarily to speak about a truer faith or a compromising of the faith in its encounter with the world or humanity. All one seeks to set forth is the manner in which aspects of this faith can be identified with aspects of society and culture that are significant for or peculiar to African-

Americans. Such elements may be significant to others as well, and they may also be required of faith qua faith. No group of believers or system of faith stands outside this process of contextualization.

My purpose in this essay is simply to indicate how African-Americans have contextualized their faith—that is, adapted it to their social, cultural, and personal situation. I shall set forth the general factors present in the creation of this distinctive version of Christianity, and then show how one very gifted African-American adapted the general tradition to some very concrete issues of liberation.

The existence of an African-American tradition within Christianity points, then, to a contextualization, just as do the designations Western Christianity, Roman Catholic Church, or Anglican Church. In every instance, the verities of the Christian faith were related to a set of historical circumstances in European, English, or American history so as to give them a relevance and specificity they might not have had were they not interpreted in the light of their import and meaning for those particular historical events. Moreover, African people had engaged in a contextualization of their faith prior to the diaspora that brought them to the Americas. Such a process took place in Ethiopia in relation to the Coptic Church and in Western, Eastern, and Southern Africa following the European incursions and invasions of the fifteenth century. African-Americans were not, then, as a people, undertaking an entirely new venture. Their forebears, as well as they themselves and many other races and peoples, had acted to contextualize their faith.

What was unusual was not the process but its involuntariness, its need to receive an almost complete culture as well as religion, and its need to discover the truths of the new culture and religion among distortions and misrepresentations of truth conveyed to them by the members of the new society and faith. Their context was not a constructive one which encouraged their acquisition of faith, but a hostile one which sought to destroy their old culture and faith, and exclude them from the culture and faith their oppressors sought to employ in order to continue their control over them. In a land dedicated to liberty, they did not enjoy freedom of person, whether their status was that of slave or freedman. In a land dedicated to freedom of religion, they were not permitted to practice publicly the religion of their native Africa, to learn without hindrance the sacred or secular scriptures of their new land, or to participate without control and discrimination in the practice of piety and worship. Contextualization for them, if it were to be constructive, required a learning and a transformation of the context and faith in which they had been placed as a result of their removal from their homeland in Africa.

In spite of the almost total control exercised over them and the continuing effort of others to define them as chattel or inferior human beings, often with a sanction based upon an interpretation of the Christian faith, African-Americans responded by using their human powers of intellect and choice to create a world for themselves. This worldview contained some elements of their former cultural, social, and religious systems but drew primarily upon the secular and sacred symbol systems extant in their new land.

They did not adopt, however, the meanings accepted by their masters and oppressors, but provided for themselves new understandings of societal values and religious faith. The new meanings developed from their own experience of their humanity and the aspirations embodied in their souls and the idealism embodied in the nation's value system. They made central in their religious understandings and their social and cultural values those beliefs that undergirded their dignity as persons and their right to possess liberties and freedoms equal to those possessed by all white persons in society.

The first aspect of contextualization of the faith introduced by the African-American was the incorporation of the idea of a transcendent God and a moral law to which the nation and its people were accountable, and which drew upon those elements of the nation's creed and the Christian faith which enabled African-Americans to assert their full humanity and to work for equality for all persons. This critical posture toward society and religion, this deep passion to actualize the recognition of all individuals as equal members of the human family of the one sovereign and universal God, persists to this day as a key position of the African-American religious tradition.

The second important aspect of the process of contextualization of the faith was the establishment of independent congregations and denominations. Whether invisible or visible, these largely autonomous institutions removed African-American religious life from the control and supervision of those who sought to use the faith as a means for controlling and dehumanizing African-Americans. They were thereby freed to develop those elements of faith that could best empower them. In addition, they were encouraged to rely completely upon their own material and religious resources for sustenance and nurturance in life. Although the necessity for these structures pointed to the corruption within the white religious communities, their creation by African-Americans pointed to the manner in which they acted to relate their faith to their own needs and how they shunned accepting a faith developed to provide divine sanction for their enslavement and segregation. Independent churches and congregations provided a greater freedom of worship and religion as well as the opportunity to devise liturgies, songs, and services of worship in an idiom suitable to the interest of the people.

Independent and relatively autonomous religious institutions enabled African-Americans to contextualize their faith in yet another fashion. These institutions nurtured the sacred worldview embodying human dignity and freedom of person, and inspired African-Americans to use their religious institutions and values as models for creating secular institutions of all kinds—educational, recreational, and social, political, economic, and charitable. These institutions served as a base for implementing the values of liberty, equality, democracy, rule of law, and love present in the ideals of the new nation but not carried out by its constitution or its Christian churches. African-American people thus contextualized their faith by using its power and influence to transform the community and situation in which they lived. They sought to actualize the dream implicit in the American ideal and to live the neighbor love proclaimed by Jesus the Christ. The color line was to be removed and democracy and Christianity were to be made accessible to red and black as well as white people.

Albert J. Raboteau in an unpublished paper, "Martin Luther King, Jr., and the Tradition of Black Religious Protest," quotes a clergyman of the African Methodist Episcopal Church, T. G. Steward, who in 1888 set forth this vision. Raboteau states:

> In his treatise, *The End of the World*, he intended to debunk Josiah Strong's paean to the mission of the Anglo-Saxon race in his book, *Our Country* (1885), by using scripture and history to demonstrate that America had been displaced in the drama of salvation. It was impossible for America to convert the world to Christianity . . . because America had turned Christianity from a world religion into a clan cult. Americans preached and practiced Anglo-Saxonism, not Christianity. Assessing the militarism, nationalism, ethnocentrism, and materialism of the time, Steward concluded that the civilization epitomized by Europeans and Americans would soon destroy itself in fratricidal warfare. A new age was about to begin, during which the darker peoples of the world, long oppressed by Western Civilization, would create a raceless, classless, weaponless Christianity that would convert the world and welcome the arrival of "the universal Christ" [Raboteau, 11-12].

By the year 1900 contextualization of the faith among African-Americans had created a new religious perspective in America that sought to practice and live a faith and democracy that affirmed the dignity and equality of all persons, to create institutions that supported that conception and which protested the status quo and sought to transform the nation's institutions so that they would conform to this new understanding of the one human family. The people's universalism and egalitarian orientation had but one serious flaw. It did not understand fully the implications of its faith for the women of the world.

This African-American approach to contextualization can be seen in action in the many movements, institutions, and conceptions of self-identity fashioned by Black Americans. Its most prominent representatives in the 1960s were the Reverend Martin Luther King, Jr., and the Southern Christian Leadership Conference as it existed under his leadership during the Civil Rights Revolution.

King acknowledged in his first book, *Stride Toward Freedom*, that he was called by the people to lead a protest they had determined to make. This grassroots initiative attests to the fact that the orientation of contextualization of the faith was widespread in the African-American tradition and that the people themselves not only lived it, but expected members of the clergy and religious associations to practice it by acting to enhance the people's dignity and to seek the full implementation of the democratic and religious values of equality professed by the nation and Christianity. King was summoned to lead the protest, in part because religious associations and the clergy were perceived to be guardians of the tradition and responsible for its actualization. The faith contextualized in their persons and community thus supported the people in their bus boycott in Montgomery and their pursuit of equal justice under law in the courts of the land.

In Montgomery King was not only an eloquent and effective spokesperson for the African-American manner of contextualizing the faith, but also one who transformed its nonviolent dimension into an active ingredient for social change. In the days that followed the success of the boycott, he continued to exhibit his critical understanding of the tradition by participating in the creation of the Southern Christian Leadership Conference, an organization that not only responded to the will of the masses, but sought to form the masses into instruments of social change. The motto of the new organization emphasized its concern "to transform the soul of America," but even more importantly that aspiration underscored King's and the group's commitment to universalism. The values of freedom and equality enunciated in the Declaration of Independence were to be made real in America. Moreover, in accomplishing this, King had linked the Christian conception of love as stated in the Sermon on the Mount to the Gandhian teaching on nonviolence implying thereby a Third World solidarity over against white supremacy and racism. The inspirational nature of the American value system had worldwide influence, but Martin Luther King, Jr., was singular in indicating to Americans how they could learn the true and full meaning of their values by reflecting on the revolutionary struggles of Third World peoples.

The occasion which imprinted this insight indelibly on King's mind was the ceremony marking the creation of Ghana as an independent nation-state. Dr. and Mrs. King attended and Martin was overwhelmed by the pageantry and symbolism of the day. In a sermon preached in Atlanta at the Ebenezer Baptist Church upon his return he remarked that the ceremony was not "an ephemeral evanescent event appearing on the stage of history. But it was an event with eternal meaning." The independence of Ghana underscored his conviction that the powers of the universe were friendly and the moral arc of the universe was bent in the direction of justice. Ghana's independence vindicated the African-American faith in God's righteousness. A new age was dawning, bringing liberation for all oppressed peoples. The American civil rights movement was, King believed, a part of this worldwide march of freedom. This orientation broadened and made more profound the African-American quest to achieve equality and dignity. The crusades in Albany, Birmingham, and Selma became vigorous struggles to transform the national ethos and not just a locality. King and other African-Americans utilized Alabama, Georgia, and Mississippi, areas similar to colonies in 1957, to bring social change in America and to raise the aspirations for freedom in the Third World.

The African-American contextualization of the faith, strengthened by the hopes attached to the creation of the United Nations and the ethos of decolonization, became in the movement led by Martin Luther King, Jr., an instrument for enunciating a conviction regarding God's concern for the dignity and equality of all persons within the social and political structures of the world as well as before God's throne. The vestiges of slavery, segregation, and colonization were to be removed and all people made free to engage in the creation of human communities, societies, and nations.

King envisioned a new age present in embryo in Africa, Asia, and Latin America. America could aid its coming to be if the nation could be prodded into abandoning its patterns of segregation and discrimination, and its African-American citizens motivated to become a vanguard for a transformed America. King sought first to implement the new age among his own people living in the legally segregated and disenfranchised southland of America. When that task was largely accomplished by the passage of the Civil Rights Acts of 1957 and 1964 and the Voting Rights Act of 1965, he turned his attention to other areas of American life—education, housing, and the economy. The agenda was the historical legacy of the African-American contextualization of the faith, but it was made multiracial and international by King's encounter with Nkrumah and Ghana and Gandhi and India. In the urban North and West matters were more difficult and less successful, but the crusade did not die and the faith was not quenched.

The African-American contextualization of the faith always involved the creation of new institutions. Under King's leadership the religious and civil community depended upon an organization, the voluntary association, that had long been prominent in the United States and in the Black community as the vehicle for change. Some have argued that the voluntary association was prior to the church as the first and basic African-American social institution. Perhaps so. In King's day the communities were overorganized in the sense that there were numerous and conflicting churches and voluntary associations—clubs, sororities, lodges, and special interest groups. The nearly universal response of the Montgomery community to the arrest and imprisonment of Rosa Parks created an atmosphere in which the community could be unified by the creation of a comprehensive and inclusive communal association capable of mobilizing all the people for protest against their most salient injustice. The Montgomery Improvement Association was successful at the metropolitan level. Others similar to it were organized in other cities.

The Southern Christian Leadership Conference incorporated these and other such organizations into a regional and then national multiracial and multifaith organization greatly influenced by the Black church's faith and culture and under the leadership of its clergy. While the Southern Christian Leadership Conference never became the sole African-American organization, it symbolized better than any other how the people's faith was contextualized and put to work on behalf not only of their own betterment but that of all peoples. King had helped to expand it from a local, to national, to multiracial protest movement. At the time of his death he was planning to use it in a poor people's campaign to reduce greatly if not end poverty.

T. G. Steward in his treatise, *The End of the World*, called upon African-Americans to "create a raceless, classless, weaponless Christianity." In one respect at least his wishes departed from their tradition. A people who knew that their freedom resulted from a civil war in which they were eager to participate and whose limited freedom was being daily threatened by white mobs did not quickly embrace a call to "weaponless Christianity." Nonviolence as a philosophy among Black Americans existed long before Gandhi and was proclaimed in a sophisticated manner by William Whipper as early as 1837. Yet it was not until Martin Luther King's campaigns that it was put forth as a necessary and essential aspect of the African-American religious tradition. The advent of Black Power, Malcolm X, and James Cone was to challenge seriously this advocacy by King.

Nonetheless, it must be noted that King persuaded many to accept his view for more than a decade and that he argued for his position in respect to the United States' involvement in the Vietnam War and nuclear warfare. He sought to contextualize the faith in such a fashion as to enable it to be true to its history and to the demands of the situation that confronted the people. Whether the people will finally accept the position set forth by him is not known. The debate continues, and the affinity of African-Americans to South African Blacks, Coloureds, and Asians, as well as to other Third World peoples, will play a large part in the outcome. What we do know is that the uncertainty indicates once more the constant and enduring concern of African-Americans to contextualize their faith.

CHAPTER 11

Survival, Hope, and Liberation in the Other American Church: An Hispanic Case Study

Orlando E. Costas

Minority churches in the United States have functioned, by and large, as places of survival and hope. This is certainly the case with the slaves brought from Africa and their descendants. In the opening pages of his well-known work, *God of the Oppressed*, James H. Cone shares what the church has meant to him as a Black man.

> The Black Church introduced me to the essence of life as expressed in the rhythm and feelings of black people in Bearden, Arkansas. At Macedonia Africa Methodist Episcopal Church (A.M.E.), I encountered the presence of the divine Spirit, and my soul was moved and filled with an aspiration for freedom. Through prayer, song, and sermon, God made frequent visits to the black community in Bearden and reassured the people of his concern for their well-being and his will to bring them safely home [Cone, 1].

He goes on to say:

> After being told six days of the week that they were nothings by the rulers of white society, on the Sabbath, the first day of the week, black people went to church in order to experience another definition of their humanity. . . . Those six days of wheeling and dealing with white people always raised the anxious questions of whether life was worth living. But when blacks went to church and experienced the presence of Jesus' Spirit among them, they realized that he bestowed a meaning upon their lives that could not be taken away by white folks. That's why folks at Macedo-

136

nia sang: "A little talk with Jesus makes it right": not that "white is right," but that God had affirmed the rightness of their existence, the righteousness of their being in the world. That affirmation enabled black people to meet "the Man" on Monday morning and to deal with his dehumanizing presence the remainder of the week, knowing that white folks could not destroy their humanity [Cone, 12–13].

The experience of Black Christians has been duplicated over and over in the life struggle of other American minority Christians. Paul Nagano, a Japanese-American Baptist minister, who as a young man had to spend two years in an American concentration camp during World War II, shared with me during a visit to his home in Seattle, Washington, how he and other Japanese Christians were able to survive and overcome such a humiliating ordeal through their faith in Jesus Christ. He left the concentration camp to attend Bethel Seminary in St. Paul, Minnesota. We can discover a similar experience in the life and story of the well-known Mexican actor, Anthony Quinn, who during his teenage years in California became a member of an emerging Pentecostal church. In his autobiography, *The Original Sin*, Quinn comments on the impact which the founder of the Four Square Gospel Church, Aimee Semple McPherson, had upon the life of Mexican immigrants during the Depression. He says that during the height of the Depression, when hunger and poverty permeated America:

> There were many Mexicans who were terrified of appealing for county help because most of them were in the country illegally. When in distress, they were comforted by the fact that they could call one of Aimee's branches at any time of the night. There, they never would be asked any of the embarrassing questions posed by the authorities. The fact that they were hungry or in need of warm clothing was enough. No one even asked if they belonged to Aimee's church or not [Quinn, 128–29].

These three testimonies suffice to demonstrate the importance of the church as a place of survival and hope for American ethnic minorities. In the course of this paper I want to examine critically the dynamics of survival and hope in the minority church. I shall do so by describing the experience of a former Puerto Rican convict in a New York Hispanic Pentecostal church. This will lead me to an analysis of the content of this case, which in turn will enable me to point out the limits of an ecclesiology of survival and hope and the need to develop a liberating ecclesiology for minority churches in general and the Hispanic church in particular.

An Hispanic Case Study:
Piri Thomas and the Rehoboth Spanish Mission Pentecostal Church

Piri Thomas is a Black Puerto Rican who was born and reared in New York City. He spent six years in Sing Sing Prison on a fifteen-year sentence for armed robbery. Out on parole, he wrote his life story in the best seller, *Down These Mean Streets*. In this book he describes his personal odyssey through delinquency, dope and prison. In a second book, *Savior, Savior, Hold My Hand*, Thomas narrates his spiritual pilgrimage and relationship to the Hispanic church. The latter is not only a beautiful example of a spiritual autobiography from the barrio, but represents a first class indigenous theological critique of what I call the "other" church in North America. This is the church of North American minorities, many of whom are to be found in the major cities of the country. The fact that they are socially and culturally connected with Africa, Asia and the Pacific, Latin America and the Caribbean, tells us that the other American church is both the North American counterpart of the church in the Two Thirds world and presents mainstream theological institutions with similar challenges. This is, therefore, the source which I shall use for the present case study.

Upon his release from prison, Piri came home to his aunt (or *tía*) in El Barrio (Spanish Harlem). She was more than an aunt; she was his substitute mother, since his own had died years before. He had been living with her when he was taken to prison. A faithful Pentecostal Christian, she received him with open arms, but reminded him where he had come from by giving him the clothes he had on when he was given his prison sentence.

No sooner had he come home than his aunt invited him to visit her Pentecostal church. For Piri the Pentecostal experience was an exotic, fascinating trip:

> The most beautiful thing about the Pentecostals was their ability to pour themselves into the power of the Holy Spirit. . . . It was a miracle how they could shut out the hot and cold running cockroaches and king-size rats and all the added horrors of decaying rotten tenement houses and garbage-littered streets, with drugs running through the veins of our ghetto kids. It was a miracle that they could endure the indignities poured upon our Barrios. I knew that everyone of them didn't get weaker. They got stronger. Their prayers didn't get shorter. They got longer. Those who looked for God to come closer were blessed with El Bautismo del Espíritu Santo, and they spoke a language that I could not understand. Tía had said it was the tongue of the angels, and only a few could interpret it.
>
> Wow, I thought to myself. If ever there were an escape this has got to be it. Is God gonna make it up to us in heaven?
>
> Caramba, I smiled, maybe it ain't an escape, maybe like a somber Pentecostal guy had once told me. Maybe, like he had said, they aren't interested in material wealth. God's Kingdom will provide enough for all in the sweet bye and bye. God's work and God's will be done. But . . . "How about starting here on earth, brother, with the nitty-gritty reality?" I had asked this Pentecostal guy. He had looked at me funny and had said, "God's Kingdom is not of this earth." "But we are," I had insisted. He just shook his head and walked away [Thomas, 17–18].

But for Piri's *tía* the church was not an escape; it was a place of survival—and hope! One day he asked her:

> "Tía? What does being a Pentecostal mean to you?" . . . Tía smiled like always, sure and secure in her iglesia . . . "It's like being part of a familia that is together in Cristo and we help each other with the little materials we may possess." She talked on about us not having silver and gold but having instead peace in our corazones and salvation as our goal [Thomas, 18].

Piri got a job and continued to visit his aunt's church. One day the sermon touched a sensitive chord in his life and he responded affirmatively to the call to confess Jesus Christ as his personal savior. He walked forward to the altar:

> This walk was nothing like I ever took. It was different. There wasn't anybody waiting at the end to hurt me. It wasn't like the long walk down El Barrio's streets on the way to a bop, or to pull a job—or holding my bloody side, stumbling and walking down that long cold street. It wasn't nothing like the long walks through the echoing Tombs—or the way to Courts—or the walk before the Big Judge. Oh, God, it wasn't like the long walk through the long years in prison through cell hall blocks and green-barred cell tiers—or the long wait and long walk to see the Wise Men, the Parole Board, and going back again after two years. It wasn't like the long walk from one prison to another, from one court to another—or the long walk to freedom with the long invisible rope around my neck held by a probation officer and a parole officer. It was unlike any of my long walks. This one hadda be for something better. This one couldn't be a blank—it hadda be for real. I was gonna be somebody after this long walk. I was gonna be a positive power—like I said—like the Big Man said—like on the kick of "Suffer the little children to come unto me" [Thomas, 68].

Piri became literally a new person as a result of this transforming experience. He began to take new steps in his Christian pilgrimage. He became part of the young people's society. He got a guitar and began writing gospel songs:

> Savior, Savior, Hold My Hand
> Lead me on to Freedom's land
> Help me try to understand
> That a man's a brother to another man.

In this and other songs Piri expressed his new found faith, which, more than a refuge, was a pilgrimage of hope, a quest for liberation and ultimate reconciliation. The Christian life was not easy. Living as a Christian in the old neighborhood was an ongoing struggle. Old friends came by; the temptation to go back to the way of easy money was a daily reality, especially when the job he had was menial. But Piri persevered, thanks to the help of his pastor and the sisters and brothers in the church.

At church he met Nita, a young devoted Christian woman. They married and began to build a Christian home.

The word soon got around the New York evangelical network that this former convict had been converted. One day Piri's pastor introduced him to a representative of the American Tract Society who wanted to consider the possibility of publishing a tract about Piri's faith-experience. Through this man, Piri came to know a Christian policeman, a captain of one of the precincts in Spanish Harlem. Piri knew the man and he knew of Piri—both before and after prison. The exchange led to another acquaintance: a former gangster and convict, John Clause, who had been converted and had since become a minister. Clause had been led to come back to the city to work with youth gangs. He saw in Piri a person who could help him develop a ministry with youth. Thus through the financial support of his Anglo, suburban church, John Clause offered Piri a job to help him reach the hard-to-reach of the barrio. At first Piri hesitated. He had lots of reservations. But after thinking it over, he decided to accept the offer. Piri entered a partnership with Clause, going to work as his associate in the ministry to teenage gangs.

Things went very well—for a while. Piri became an effective street worker— a true peacemaker in the same neighborhood where he had once been a lawbreaker. The youth club flourished and the news of its successful approach with hard-to-reach youth began to spread all over the country as the Christian media carried the story to the evangelical public.

Then trouble began to creep into the relationship between Piri and the kids he was working with, and with Clause and the type of Christianity he represented. Here is how Piri tells it:

> Things began to change between me and a certain brand of Christianity. That pink cloud of togetherness was beginning to dissolve. I had noticed things I hadn't dug before or perhaps hadn't wanted to dig in the white Christian/ghetto relationship. It was like we weren't equals. It was as if they were the chosen ones—despite the teaching in their Bibles—like they were sent to save us by getting us a hearing with Christ. But like it had to be on their own terms . . . I realized . . . what a difference there was between our storefront churches in El Barrio and this [church] . . . Like ours are poor in bread, but really rich in spirit and this was just rich in pesos [Thomas, 234].

Not only did Piri detect a lot of hypocrisy in John Clause's brand of Christianity, but also a strong dose of paternalism and blatant racism. Indeed he discovered that the so-called partnership was nothing more than a relationship of ministerial inequality.

Things came to a head when Clause kicked out of the club a 14-year-old kid for swearing and threatening one of the white volunteer workers, and then made Piri turn him in to the police. Piri felt that "Chiquito," as the kid was called, was unjustly crucified:

> I left the precinct very quietly . . . and let my feet take me on some kind of walking while my mind went on some kind of flying that had mucho to do with John's attitudes. Diggit, John, I thought, you can't handle people's lives like they were wooden puppets. God, no wonder I use to feel uncomfortable everytime I've gone to your house. Your wife and kids would walk tippy-toes around the house like as if they were afraid to breathe. Diggit, John, like anything you said was law, you roared at them the same way you did at Chiquito. I ain't got no doubts you provide for them mucho good up in that pretty house, but you sure hand them some kind of hardbrand love. [Man]! you may rule your house with some way-out iron fist, but here in our Barrio, we're tired of being pressured by all kinds of half-ass white rulers. Diggit, John, I hate your guts and am damn sure you hate mine. But why is it that you haven't fired me, John? Don't tell me. Let me guess. Yeah, it's because you can use me [Thomas, 290].

Thereafter it was just a matter of days until Piri quit his job. He called John Clause up one day and told him loud and simple: "I quit. Like you aren't for real. . . . I'm a human being, John. I ain't no broom in a corner . . . it's game time now. . . . Pure and simple, I quit" (Thomas, 302).

Piri took on a secular job, but he returned to his old church in the barrio. He got himself involved in its ministry, but by this time he had grown too much in his social consciousness. Little by little he became disillusioned with the church. Nita, his wife, realized it, and asked him, "Honey, are you getting cold with God?" Piri answered:

> "Honey, I'm not cold with God . . . I'm just frozen to death by the hypocrisy. Come here," I said, . . . "Dig, corazon, what's the use of me going to church seven days a week and praying and singing while our Barrio is swinging with all kinds of miseries? No amount of praying and singing is gonna change these ten hundred pounds of calluses on their knees in going in prayer to the Lord for a way out from all the poverty and exploitation. Diggit, Nita, prayer is good for the soul. Singing to God is good for the spirit. But putting into action the changes that gotta be made is most chevere for the body, and that's where it's at, Nita. We're physical beings also and I personally don't believe in having to go to heaven in order to at last live right.
>
> If we love one another, God dwelleth in us, and his love is perfected in us. Like that's where it's at, Nita. I believe the true salvation of us ghetto people is when we get together in one solid fist and smash down the walls of . . . hypocrisy. Honey, I've seen more brother and sisterhood in our

nitty-gritty people than in any of those great golden temples. Honey, our people are living in misery and still are kissing a finger with a great diamond ring on it and calling its owner FATHER. . . . We cover our eyes with God and become content to live in these damn conditions. I know Christ is great, honey. I just wish he'd come down and walk with us nitty-gritty.

Baby, I'm not putting God down. I'm just wondering why the hell we've allowed certain people to put us down. I can't carry no cross and be nailed to it at the same damned time. Wow, honey, don't you dig that to us people of the Barrio the ghetto is our church, and the only way we're gonna make a heaven out of this hell is by getting together?" [Thomas, 325–26,327].

Thus Piri ended up leaving the church.

What had gone wrong? Was the problem with Piri? Was it with John Clause and his Anglo Christian friends? Or was it with the Hispanic church?

Certainly there was in Piri a trace of social dechristianization: he ended up making a commitment to people in the barrio and rejecting the institutional church. But the real problem was with both the Anglo and barrio churches. The Anglo church, represented in John Clause, was a symbol of paternalism and hypocrisy. The Hispanic church was a place of survival rather than liberating hope. In a word, it was a place of personal solidarity with a marginalized people, but not an agent of social liberation in an oppressed community. This becomes evident once we sort out the content of Piri's experience.

A Meditation on Survival and Hope: Sorting out the Content

The case of Piri Thomas and the Rehoboth Spanish Mission Pentecostal Church enables us to reflect critically on the role of the minority church in its surrounding community. Indeed it helps us to identify its value and limitations as a place of survival and hope. There are several dimensions of survival present in this case. First, there is the dimension of psychological survival. The church of the barrio is a place where people like Piri and his aunt can find personal meaning; they become somebody. They can be themselves—sing, shout, pray, cry, create, even dream—without being harassed and ridiculed. There they experience God and find themselves accepted by the trinitarian community: they discover that they are not orphans but children of the heavenly Father; that they are not helpless, because Jesus, their big brother, is now near to them; and that their sadness, fears, and anxieties are replaced by the joy, certainty, and hope of the Spirit. Thus they are able to recover their heart—indeed their personal humanity.

The barrio church also enables its members to survive culturally. It keeps alive their language, which is an essential tool for cultural survival. Language preserves and transmits the "spirit" of any culture. In churches like Rehoboth people can worship God in their own tongue. They can preserve the Hispanic/

Puerto Rican tradition (even if in a broken and tarnished manner) and transmit it to new generations. Moreover such churches give their members a religious language which enables them to express the unexpressable and to articulate the undescribable. They thus become part of a subculture whose chief trait is enabling people to have a cultural identity. That is why Rehoboth became the central place in the lives of its members: they went to church seven days a week, not because they did not have other things to do, but rather because the church was their life, the only place where they could express an authentic and free mode of being.

The barrio church also provides the space for social survival. In it poor people experience solidarity. They care for and look after each other. Thus, for example, Piri found his first major job through a member of the church. Being so near to each other's reality, it is natural for parishioners to develop a poor-people's consciousness. This is why when John Clause took Piri and members of the youth club to a large church in downtown Manhattan, Piri noticed immediately the difference between the latter and the storefront churches in El Barrio: "ours are poor in bread, but really rich in spirit, and this was just rich in pesos," he commented.

Besides highlighting the reality of survival in the minority church, the case considered discloses a horizon of hope. Indeed it reveals a people who go on living because they anticipate a far better future. In the barrio they suffer economic hardship and downright injustice. They live in crowded and run-down apartments, breathe unclean air, send their children to overcrowded, understaffed and poorly kept schools; they walk through unclean and unsafe streets; they work in low-paying jobs. They often cannot help wondering why others have over and beyond their needs while they can hardly make it. But in church they hear the promise of the gospel:

> Blessed are you poor,
>   for yours is the kingdom of God.
> Blessed are you that hunger now,
>   for you shall be satisfied.
> Blessed are you that weep now,
>   for you shall laugh [Luke 6:20–21].

In church, minority Christians are fed the hope of shalom; they look forward to a new earth and new heavens. They anticipate the day when justice will be done at last, when God will wipe away all tears, take away their hunger, give them space to live and live well, and death will be done away with.

In the barrio, minority Christians live in a state of powerlessness. They have no control over the streets, the schools, the economy, their environment. They are victims of a powerful consumer society. They are reduced to a passive resistance. But in church they are empowered by the Spirit to speak the truth, to heal the rotten body, bring hope to desperate souls, and set free those that are demon-possessed. In church they become participants in the drama of history,

God's agents in the redemption of the universe, representatives before God of their barrios, and indeed of the whole world.

In church minority Christians relativize temporal powers. They grasp the ultimate meaning of all human histories. They cease to be intimidated by the powers of this world—whether political or economic, social or cultural. They are set free because they encounter the Lord present in the Spirit, and where the Spirit of the Lord is, there is freedom—freedom from the ambiguity and predicament of history, freedom for the God who transcends all human lords and human thought, and for the world which God has promised in Christ, beyond injustice, oppression, and death.

Not everything is positive and glorious in the minority church, however. The case of Piri Thomas and the Rehoboth Spanish Pentecostal Church reveals a very serious limitation typical of most minority churches. By being a place of survival and hope, the minority church has rightly accentuated the role of religion as protest and utopia, but it has also truncated its transformational possibilities. Thus Rehoboth helped Piri to survive and transcend the limitations of his environment, but it did not help him to transform it. There Piri learned to hope even when there seemed to be no hope, to pray even if God seemed far removed from him, and to sing the Lord's song when he knew that he was in a strange land. But when he wanted to translate that hope into concrete action for the barrio, the world where God had set the Rehoboth church to serve, he was left stranded.

The problem with this and other minority churches is that they interiorize their experience of liberation. Indeed they lack a historical project—a future direction broad enough not to get bogged down with the difficulties of developing specific programs of social transformation, and specific enough so as not to evaporate into the eschatological vision of a world beyond. This is in fact what Piri was asking for, but the church did not, and probably could not, provide it, at least not without experiencing a transformation in its own self-understanding.

What the Hispanic church needs (and for that matter all minority churches) is nothing short of an ecclesiology of liberation. The Hispanic church needs to develop a vision of itself and its mission beyond survival and hope. Indeed, it needs an ecclesiology which will free it from introversion, other-worldliness and churchism, free it for mission, incarnation, and the kingdom of God. This is the enormous task that lies before the emerging generation of Hispanic pastors and theologians.

References

Cone, James. 1975. *God of the Oppressed*. New York: Seabury.
Quinn, Anthony. 1972. *The Original Sin: Self-Portrait*. Boston: Little, Brown and Co.
Thomas, Piri. 1972. *Savior, Savior, Hold My Hand*. New York: Bantam Books.

CHAPTER 12

Theological Education in the Urban Context

Douglas Hall

Urban training needs to come from the interests and long-term needs of urban people. It should model what it teaches, first of all, by not being just another event that uses the city, but rather is used by the city and its people for their own spiritual and social needs and purposes. It is too easy for an educational institution to feel that it should have an urban training program and proceed to put one together. The temptation is to want to talk intelligently about the topic, rather than to perform the tasks that amount to doing biblical Christianity in the city. Urban training needs to be a part of the answer, not a part of the problem. Otherwise the complexity of the urban environment could render our efforts not only nonproductive but even counterproductive. And if our efforts are counterproductive over the long run, the question can honestly be asked, "Whose side are we on?"

A Theology That Sees the City as a Strategic Environment for Christian Ministry

The city and its people have an infinite array of needs, and ministry must address these needs relevantly, but to do so it must see the environment first of all as a strategic one for ministry, and not simply as needs.

The strategy of the apostle Paul was to impact the city, and many of the letters of the New Testament reflect this focus by bearing the names of ancient cities. The message of the gospel was to begin in the capital city of a subservient Hebrew nation and spread to its entire region and then to the world (Acts 1:8). Help was requested by the poor saints of Jerusalem, but the clear strategy of mission in the first century was not merely to help the city. Simply sending help can become a very paternal, nondevelopmental approach, and such approaches help only initially and in geographically limited ways. The city networks almost everything that is in it, for good or for evil. Social problems such as drugs and family breakup, once associated with inner cities, are problems everywhere today. When the spiritual and social needs of people in cities are met, we will have already begun to meet the future needs of people living in the suburbs. As churches die in cities they eventually begin to die in concentric rings around cities.

When we see these realities and become concerned for our posterity and our region over the long run, we must be concerned to train people to take the city very seriously. Our Christian future demands that we train them as best we can, under God, best to perform as productively as possible for the kingdom of God. We cannot thus simply be training people to hold things together in a dying church, but we must be training them to build existing churches and plant new ones. The social ministry of the church must be at its most mature level in cities. By "mature" I mean existing in very healthy indigenous church and parachurch systems, and meeting needs in a way that also develops existing communities. When we begin to do this in cities, we well know how to do it anywhere; in fact, we will almost automatically do it in the nonurban areas, most of which are affected by cities. Paul followed his missionary vision of Macedonia by going directly to its capital city of Philippi (Acts 16:9-12).

Realities Experienced in the Urban Environment

Students of the city must be prepared spiritually and psychologically, socially and strategically, to minister in an area that is complex, heterogeneous, dynamic, and manipulative.

1. *Urban complexity requires that pastors be trained in the basics of socio-cultural systems, and that they fit into a ministry that seeks to be effective over the long run.*

a. Training in the basics. Cities have their political and dynamic delivery systems that are both complex and numerous. A seminary training program must inform students about these areas, but can only begin to touch the surface. Students must be trained on how to research their environment and have tools so they can use its systems, but a seminary does not have the luxury to train extensively in these areas. The program I am involved in, though stressing the above concerns, is based on a social analysis theory that focuses on conceptual constructs basic to all social environments. For example, we teach how to research and carry on social and spiritual ministry in (1) primary systems—that is, systems that meet needs via the relational networks of family, extended family, ethnic community, and the natural interrelationships found in more intimate neighborhood communities; and (2) secondary systems, which meet needs via organizational and economic types of interaction. The job often involves building the former systems up and making the latter system operate justly. The poor normally function better in primary systems than in the secondary systems. The most vital forms of Christianity often exist among the poor in many cities. Therefore ministry to the poor is vital from the social justice perspective, and from the perspective of strategy as well.

b. *Gearing our ministry to the long-term concerns.* Jay Forrester, in his book, *Urban Dynamics*, tells us that "change in a complex system commonly causes short-term responses in the opposite direction from the long-term effect" (Forrester, 112). Thus, if we are to accomplish goals that have long-term effects, long-term involvement is often a prerequisite, or at least, having involvements which have good follow-up systems. I often tell my students, "If it falls apart after you leave, it does not show how important you were, but how unimportant." Sometimes our own need to be needed can contribute to a very negative result in the city. Self-centered involvements do not belong in urban ministry.

2. *Urban heterogeneity requires that cross-cultural training be a central concern in all legitimate urban training programs.* It is all too possible for people who are even well-trained in cross-cultural concerns in overseas situations to operate inappropriately in urban efforts in this regard. Cognitive knowledge must be followed up by supervised experiences, and even then some people more naturally have this gift than do others. An absolute need is that those who plan to minister to another culture must positively care about those people, be able to have effective communication with them, and understand how they perceive their own needs before even attempting to think about relevant ministry to them.

3. *Cities are dynamic; therefore training programs must develop the student's ability to do analysis before applying learned methods.* Eighty percent of a particular population of a city can change in two years, and this is only one of many changing urban dynamics. Methods that work in one part of a city at one time will not necessarily work there two years later (motion pictures of events and buildings in neighborhood areas may seem like ancient history shown even three years later). We, therefore, cannot be heavy on teaching a lot of specific methods and techniques. Future ministers need to be taught how to analyze communities and their situations regularly. Problems often need to be anticipated because relevant ministry often has a significant tooling-up period, and the need for what you are planning may be over by the time you are ready to do something. Or the need may have become too critical by that time to have any basic effect on causal factors. Not all cities are changing rapidly, but all cities are changing.

4. *City populations often feel very manipulated by many dynamics in their environments,* such as the dynamic of change just mentioned. The poor, particularly, are manipulated and thus are very leery of new plans designed to benefit them. In this regard indigenously developed programs are by far the best. Even the designing of an urban training program for the city by a seminary will itself often be seen as a threat to that urban area; cooperation will be very slow in coming from urban people. Therefore, the best and most long-term urban training programs are those that have been asked for and developed by urban people who work with a seminary to design these

programs, and the seminary responds by training and assisting those who want to do the job, rather than by initiating or mobilizing the city for the seminary's agenda.

Realities of the Working Environment in and through Which the Urban Practitioner Ministers

1. *The person who ministers needs to be analyzed in an urban training program.* Burn-out is very common, and often is due to personality and family factors apart from the actual environmental pressures. We encourage spouses to attend classes because marital disunity can be one of the major factors in failure in urban ministry. A personal analysis is always done by students and reviewed by friends, supervisor, and faculty in the program in which I am involved. Our program requires a major paper on urban ministry where the salient aspects of an urban ministry are looked at from a student's perspective. We teach experimentation on paper rather than experimentation on people. These papers are often very practical tools for both evaluation and ministry planning.

2. *The organization through which ministry is performed needs to be looked at by those who plan to do urban ministry.* The limitations and assets of particular organizations, denominations, and churches need to be known. This is often overlooked by those who have idealized notions regarding ministry in the city. Understanding these working structures has a lot to do with setting proper expectations for the practitioner. This is a major concern in setting up a long-term ministry involvement designed to make significant contributions to the kingdom of God in the urban environment.

3. *The community and its analysis is central to relevant ministry in an urban context.* This topic was the most frequently mentioned by past students now in urban ministry as needing to be focused on in any urban ministry training. It is almost impossible to conceive how long-term church growth can occur in a typical urban neighborhood without continual and relevant interaction with the people and structures of the major contextualized community. This must be taught in such a way that the information is gathered and processed both via data and personal involvement interactions. A training program needs to enable students to make use of this information in their ministry development. Parachurch involvement needs people who can do a program and analyze data to tell them what to be doing to prepare for future ministry.

4. *Showing the importance of an ongoing study of models of ministry is critical in urban training.* Most enduring and creatively successful urban programs involve themselves in the study of ministry models in either a formal or informal manner. There are many methods utilized in studying models, but the stress often needs to be on what can easily be done by a practitioner later on in ministry. The dynamics of ministry do not often afford the time to do extremely detailed studies, and thus is far too important an exercise to be done only in the classroom and not in the field.

A Strategic Theology of Training Designed for Complex Environments

The experience of Lent has much to teach us about the dynamics of urban training. Our Lord, according to John 1, came into an environment that seemed opposed to his involvement, or at best did not understand him or his purpose. "The light shines in the darkness but the darkness has not understood it." The early events of Mark's Gospel, in the first three chapters, describe a counterproductive process, and it all is prefixed by "the beginning of the gospel about Jesus Christ, the Son of God."

Cities are often not receptive places for the development of Christianity, and those who would minister there will often have a Lenten experience in their ministry. In my own training I spend a lot of time initially bursting bubbles and showing how the complex environment of a city can work counterproductively despite our very best intentions. Our students need to be brought to the point of crying out: "You keep showing us what won't work. Well, is there anything that does?" At that point in the learning process, students are ready to be taught about urban ministry. Our training too often focuses only on learning and not enough on the humbling experience of unlearning. Generally speaking, we are not naturally prepared to do urban ministry. An urban training program must teach unlearning. It must prepare us for the difficult. Salvation comes to us personally when we face the reality of our sin and limitations, and cry out to our Lord for his mercy and help. There is productive ministry on the other side of the cross, but a part of us has been left in front of the cross, and we now go forward not as persons totally competent in ourselves. We have not simply been trained; we have been discipled.

PART SIX

A TEXT IN CONTEXT

CHAPTER 13

A Prophetic Reconception of God for Our Time

Talata Reeves

"Every group of people, every race, thinks about God out of its own state of being, its own understanding of itself. Out of its own condition of life" (Wilmore, 89). These words spoken by Gayraud S. Wilmore on the topic of Black theology adequately define the intent if not the process of contextualization. Throughout the history of the Christian church, men and women have been involved in the ongoing process of understanding the scriptures in their particular historical contexts.

Contextualization, then, is not new to the church. Indeed, the longevity of a system of belief is to some extent determined by its ability to respond to the changes in its environment. From a theological perspective, Christianity has survived because it is the will of God. Practically, it has survived because in it men and women have been able to identify its voice addressing the specifics of their times.

Contextualization has been defined by the Theological Education Fund:

Contextualization has to do with how we assess the peculiarity of the Third World contexts. Indigenization tends to be used in the same sense of responding to the Gospel in terms of a traditional culture. Contextualization, while not ignoring this, takes into account the process of secularism, technology, and the struggle for human justice, which characterize the historical moment of nations in the Third World [Theological Education Fund, 20].

Recognition of cultural differences and uniqueness that groups bring to the Christian faith is but one aspect of this process. Contextualization is dynamic interaction between the context and the text (scripture): dialogue between the ever-changing context and the changeless text. It is dynamic because the text has the peculiar quality of being both changeless and God-breathed—alive and therefore always relevant to the context (2 Tim 3:16). It is not the text that is conformed but the context which is transformed through its dialogue with the text. Contextualization should not be understood as making God's word relevant, but the process through which we come to recognize and understand God's ever-relevant word for the ever-changing historical context.

In light of this, contextualization as it pertains to mission is not the removal of culture from the scriptures but rather the incorporation of culture in the expression and life of Christians. Scripture is presented to us in its own historical contexts, human culture being one of the avenues through which our Creator has chosen to be revealed. Therefore, to present the gospel outside its original context would be to present no gospel at all. To a large extent the problem is hermeneutical. Since God's Word is ever-relevant, by what method should one interpret this Word—God's purpose for, and response to, the challenges of any historical context?

It is in this process that we are all engaged, even as the prophets were before us. Throughout Israel's turbulent history, the prophet was the lens through which Israel was consistently given the opportunity to view itself as seen through the eyes of God—and therefore as it really was. In addition, the prophetic message provided a focus for a people gone astray. The prophet of Yahweh, through his or her message, brought to God's people God's divine purpose for them. This message was not restricted to the religious sphere but concerned every aspect (socio-political, cultic, and the like) of its life at any given point in time. The purpose of the message was to call Israel back to fellowship with its God and to make clear God's will for its life. For this reason it was not always a message of hope but more often one of judgment.

Efforts toward contextualization, through the various theological perspectives espoused, exemplify the relevancy of the prophetic message in our century. We all desire and consciously pursue a faith that can speak to our individual conditions as well as to the world in which we live. The socio-political situation in Latin America and South Africa has forced the peoples of those regions to formulate a position from which they are able to function, from their own understanding, as a people of God. The same can be said for the Black experience in America. It was religious fervor for justice and righteousness, particularly as personified in Martin Luther King, Jr., that propelled him into the role of a modern-day prophet: calling America to repentance and to come to terms with the inconsistencies of its society.

What we need today is another prophet of the caliber of Isaiah, Jeremiah, or Amos—a prophet who can provide a central message of God's will for God's people in the twenty-first century. Lacking that, it becomes necessary to return to the prophetic tradition—not for lack of alternatives, but because of the nature of the prophetic tradition itself. The Israelite perception of prophecy, even if not fulfilled in the immediate sense, was that it remained relevant and significant beyond the time in which it was initially addressed:

The time when and by which it reached fulfillment were Jahweh's concern; man's part was to see that the word was handed down. And we notice particularly that even the prophecies which had plainly found their historical goal, and had thus clearly been fulfilled, were retained as prophecies which concerned Israel and could always have fresh meaning extracted from them [von Rad, 1962:45].

Therefore, for us, the message of the prophets is still able to provide fresh conclusions for the crises of our times and an understanding of Yahweh's will for and relationship with a covenanted people.

This paper postulates a prophetic reconception of God, through the message of the prophets, specifically Amos 5:18-20, to address the times in which we live. And in doing so it suggests a biblical framework within which contextualization of the faith should operate:

Woe to you who earnestly desire the Day of the Lord. Why do you long for the Day of the Lord? It will be a day of darkness not light.

As a man who flees from the mouth of a lion only to meet with a bear and goes into the house and leans his hand against the wall only to have a serpent bite him.

Is not the Day of the Lord darkness and not light? Darkness with no light in it? [Amos 5:18-20, NIV].

During the early part of the eighth century BCE, the northern kingdom under the reign of Jeroboam II enjoyed a period of peace and prosperity. Israel experienced a social revolution, moving from a relatively economically homogeneous society to one differing sharply between rich and poor. Israel enjoyed prosperity not known since the days of Solomon (Bright, 258-260). However, this political and economic upside was accompanied by a downside— injustices against the economically and socially powerless among Israel. Within this two-class system, the rich benefited at the expense of the poor. It was a system in which slaves, foreigners, orphans, and widows—the voiceless —had no one to plead their case and uphold their just claims in the courts (Amos 2:7; 5:11, 12). Social decay was accompanied by an emphasis on religious expression, rather than substance (Bright, 261-62). In such a time, Amos was sent to preach repentance and prophesy doom if Israel refused once more to respond to the divine mandate.

Employing the genre of a woe-cry, Amos demonstrates the inevitability of Israel's fate in a tale of a man who, having escaped both a lion and a bear, returns to the safety of his home—and is bitten by a serpent. It concludes with a rhetorical question: "Is not the day of the Lord darkness and not light?" Contrary to popular belief, the Day of the Lord will not be a day of sorrow for the nations, but for Israel. On that day, Israel will no longer hold its esteemed place at the side of Yahweh but share in the fate of the nations; it will be a day of darkness, not light.

The origin of the concept of the Day of Yahweh (Day of the Lord) is still debated. There is widespread disagreement among scholars concerning not only its origin, but content and interpretation. The problem is compounded by the fact that there are only a few Old Testament passages that specifically mention "Day of Yahweh." Interpretations of this concept range from an eschatological event to an historical one; from an act of judgment to one of deliverance; and from a cosmic event to one that is geographically limited. At one end of the spectrum, von Rad places the Day of Yahweh within the holy war tradition of Israel (von Rad, 1959:103). At the opposite end, Mowinckel places its origin within the temple cult of Israel as a part of the festival of Yahweh (Mowinckel, 145).

The variety of interpretations renders the task of defining the components and players on this "day" almost impossible if it is not considered in its own historical context, making it imperative that the passage in which the concept is expressed be understood as nearly as possible in its larger historical context. Indeed, the apparent disparity in content and interpretation of this concept can be attributed to the ever-changing factors of the larger historical context. A comparative study of the passages that specifically mention the Day of Yahweh reveals the following elements: (1) judgment; (2) battle; (3) natural disorders; (4) theophanic occurrences; (5) nations; and (6) establishment of a new order.

The element of judgment is consistent with this concept. Judgment is meted out to sinners in general, to nations, and to Israel:

> See, the Day of the Lord is coming, a cruel day, with wrath and fierce anger to make the land desolate and destroy the sinners within it [Isaiah 13:9].
>
> I will punish the world for its evil, the wicked for their sins [Isaiah 13:11a].

Judgment is achieved through battle. The battle is led by Yahweh who precedes his army. Destruction through warfare is one of the ways by which Yahweh judges the sinful nations:[1]

> The Lord thunders at the head of his army, his forces are beyond number and mighty are those who obey his command [Joel 2:11].

Hosts of enemies, usually belonging to the wicked nations, are also present—usually fleeing in haste (Jer. 46:5, etc.). Natural disorders and theophanies are an integral part of the Day, signifying the presence of Yahweh and the involvement of the cosmos in the divine struggle and victory over evil personified in the wicked nations. They include the darkening of the elements; stars falling down; and the skies being rolled back like a scroll (Jer. 10:10; Nahum 1:5; Ps. 46:6; etc.). Yahweh is described as thundering at the head of his army and roaring in Zion (Joel 2:11; 3:14).

On that day there is a sharp difference in the experiences of the wicked nations and the people of Yahweh. For the nations there is panic, flight, fear, trembling, and total destruction; the nations will be utterly destroyed (Jer. 46:10; Isa. 34:2, 3). Conversely, the people of Yahweh enjoy divine protection and security. Their blessings will be peace and prosperity in the presence of Yahweh in Zion, ushering in a new age in which they have a privileged role (Joel 3:16, 18).

In light of this evidence, the message of the prophet is more striking. Israel's security is not security at all. Having escaped harm from the outside, perhaps from the nations, the Israelites meet destruction in the safety of their own homes. Even they would not escape judgment on that day. For this reason, Amos questions their longing for the Day of Yahweh. It is clear that the popular belief regarding destruction on the Day of Yahweh applied only to the nations. However, the theme of responsibility resulting in judgment or prosperity is articulated throughout the prophets and is an integral part of Yahweh's covenant with the sons and daughters of Abraham (Ezek. 7:13; Amos 4:6–12, Deut. 28).

The central message that Amos delivered to Israel pertained to the justice of Yahweh. The God of Israel was not satisfied with the outward appearance of righteousness, which found its expression in religious acts. Yahweh did not belong to Israel; it was Israel who belonged to Yahweh. Therefore, Yahweh would not turn away from the injustices Israel engaged in against the weaker in Israelite society. Yahweh's desire was for justice and righteousness to characterize the Israelites. If they were to bear Yahweh's name they should exemplify Yahweh's character to the nations. Justice and righteousness must infuse the very fabric of their lives personally and socio-politically, as well as in their expression of worship. Yahweh's love for the Israelites was not the issue. Indeed, it was Yahweh's love that called them to repentance and a renewed relationship. Through Amos, Yahweh called Israel, collectively and individually, back to covenant relationship.

From the standpoint of the text, with the exception of prediction, the prophet did not introduce new information but reinterpreted the text for a new context. To understand a prophetic reconception of God we must return to the text with the following presuppositions: (1) scripture, as text, defines the concept of God and determines the framework for contextualization; (2) addressing the context is not optional to Christians but essential if we are to fulfill the great commission; and (3) prophetic tradition is alive and well through individuals engaged, as the prophets were, in contextualization.

The works and lives of Dietrich Bonhoeffer, Martin Luther King, Jr., and Bishop Desmond Tutu, modern prophets of the Christian church, exemplify the synthesis of faith and praxis. Nowhere in the prophets is this expressed more concisely than in the sixth chapter of Micah:

He has showed you, O man, what is good. And what does the Lord require of you? To act justly and to love mercy and to walk humbly with your God [Micah 6:8].

The character of the Christian life is multidimensional because it involves relationship with the Creator through Jesus Christ—"walking humbly with your God"—and relationship with fellow human beings—"to act justly and love mercy." Since creation, God has desired fellowship with men and women. It was God who sought Sarah and Abraham and their seed, to become God's special people. God sent prophets to call the Israelites back to fellowship with God and right relationship with one another. This multidimensional aspect is expressed in the New Testament in the words of Jesus Christ: "Love the Lord your God with all your heart and with all your soul and with all your mind. . . . Love your neighbor as yourself" (Matt. 22:37, 39). One without the other results in the religious schizophrenia that characterizes our times.

A major factor contributing to this condition is the prevailing concept of God. With the movement of the theological pendulum away from the Old Testament God, often misrepresented as stern and in some cases tyrannical, to the New Testament God of love, the essential character of divine justice has been underemphasized or completely ignored. God is Love. Unfortunately, love is understood not in terms of the divine but in a human context. From this standpoint, love degenerates to a self-centered relationship between God and the individual. The Creator becomes the property of the creature. As in the northern kingdom, confidence in Yahweh's love encouraged a self-centered faith that lacked a moral and ethical mandate, contrary to God's design for the people. One of the predominant characteristics of Yahweh in the prophets is God's justice. God's justice, writes Abraham Heschel, "is not an inference, but an a priori to biblical faith, self-evident: not an added attribute to His essence, but given with the very thought of God. It is inherent in His essence and identified with His way" (Heschel, 199–200).

Conversely, scripture is understood by some only in terms of justice. Social action is no longer the result of a proper relationship with Jesus Christ but replaces Christ as the means of salvation. However, it is the personal relationship with Christ through the text which determines one's ability to interact effectively in and out of cultural and geographical boundaries. Although it is true that God is love and that God loves all human beings, this divine love does not compromise divine justice. Justice is the result of divine love even as divine love compels just action. True love of God results in obedience (John 14:18), sowing the seed that enables us to love others. This love then finds its expression in seeking justice for and behaving justly toward one another. This synthesis of God's justice, tempered with mercy and love, finds its ultimate expression on the cross—mercy, because God recognized humankind's inability to pay the penalty for sin; justice, because the price had to be paid, if not by the sinner then by another; and love because God sent the Son, Jesus Christ, to pay the price for our sins. Through him all people gained access to divine adoption and eternal life.

The primary task of the church is missions, the making of disciples for Jesus Christ. Even today, the major obstacle to this commission has been the culture not of the disciple but the discipler. Contextualization must emphasize the inner struggle of the discipler to recognize cultural limitations in understanding and communicating the gospel. In addition, this process must acknowledge that cultures differ in their concepts of God and life, requiring other forms of expression and understanding. Through the Holy Spirit we are given the ability to be ministers to the nations—"becoming all things to all people."

Note

1. Discussion of battle imagery as it pertains to militarism is beyond the scope of this paper. Warfare in the scriptures should always be considered in its historical context.

References

Bright, John. 1981. *A History of Israel,* 3rd ed. Philadelphia: Westminster.

Heschel, Abraham J. 1962. *The Prophets,* 2 vols. New York: Harper and Row.

Mowinckel, Sigmund. 1954. *He That Cometh.* Nashville: Abingdon.

Theological Education Fund. 1972. *Ministry in Context.* Kent, England: New Life Press.

von Rad, Gerhard. 1962. *Old Testament Theology,* 2 vols. New York: Harper and Row.

———. April 1959. "The Origin of the Concept of the Day of Yahweh," *Journal of Semitic Studies,* vol. 4.

Wilmore, Gayraud S. 1972. "Black Theology," in *Best Black Sermons,* 6th ed. William M. Philpot, ed. Valley Forge: Judson Press.

Contributors

Festus A. Asana is a minister of the Presbyterian Church in Cameroon and former principal of the Presbyterian Theological College at Nyasoso.

Francis X. Clooney, S. J., is assistant professor of comparative theology at Boston College. He is a former teacher at the Jesuit High School for Buddhist and Hindu young men in Katmandu, Nepal.

Ruy O. Costa is the coordinator of the International Mission and Ecumenism Program of the Boston Theological Institute and is adjunct professor of Social Ethics and Missiology at the Centro para la Educación Ministerial Urbana in Boston.

Orlando E. Costas is academic dean and Judson Professor of Missiology at the Andover Newton Theological School. He has written extensively on missiology and issues related to Latin America and to Hispanic communities in the United States.

Barbara Darling-Smith is assistant to the director of the Boston University Institute for Philosophy and Religion and teaches at Bridgewater State College and Curry College in the areas of religion and philosophy.

Paul Deats is Walter G. Muelder professor of Social Ethics, Emeritus, at Boston University School of Theology and a retired minister of the United Methodist Church. Between 1978 and 1987 he and his wife, Ruth, traveled extensively in Central and South America and the Caribbean, including two study seminars in Cuba in 1980 and 1982.

Jeanne Gallo is a Central American advocate and Human Rights activist. She is a member of the faculty of the Women's Theological Center in Boston, teaching in the areas of social ethics and social analysis.

Alice Hageman is an attorney in a community law office in the Roxbury section of Boston. A Presbyterian minister, she has been co-pastor of the Church of the Covenant in Boston and has taught at the Harvard Divinity School and Seminario Evangélico de Teología, Matanzas, Cuba. She made her tenth trip to Cuba in June of 1985.

Douglas Hall is executive director of the Emmanuel Gospel Center in Boston and adjunct professor of urban ministry and long-term church-growth at Gordon-Conwell Theological Seminary.

Jane Cary Peck is associate professor of religion and society at Andover Newton Theological School and a former visiting professor at the Seminario Bíblico Latinoamericano in San José, Costa Rica.

Talata Reeves is director of the department of education of Christians for Urban Justice and adjunct professor of Old Testament at the Center for Urban Ministerial Education of Gordon-Conwell Theological Seminary.

Lucien Richard, O.M.I., is professor of systematic theology at Weston School of Theology. He has published books and articles on spirituality, world religions, and Christology.

Max Stackhouse is Gezork professor of Christian social ethics at Andover Newton Theological School. He is the co-author of *Apologia: Contextualization, Globalization, and Mission in Theological Education.*

Francis Patrick Sullivan, S.J., a poet and a theologian, teaches courses on aesthetics and theology at Boston College and at the Gregorian University in Rome. Presently he is translating the short tracts of Bartolomé de las Casas into English.

Preston N. Williams is Houghton professor of theology and contemporary change at Harvard Divinity School and chair of the Boston Theological Institute Race Relations Committee. He is a member of the Advisory Board of the Martin Luther King, Jr., Papers.